D1105558

Frank Lloyd Wright
& Lewis Mumford

Dear Llewis: A clipping of your letter to the Times shows you back again on the trail so worthy of you - and you worthy of it. A splendid courageous arraignment of gross stupidity in high places.

TALIESIN WEST

Affection,

Frank Lloyd Wright

April 5th, 1954

courtesy Frank Lloyd Wright Foundation

4002 Locust St
Long Island City
29 March 1951

Dear FLW:

Your telegram was totally unexpected: for if ever there was a labor of love my talk that night was such. But I appreciate your generosity & will not make you uncomfortable by questioning it. Enough if I say, very sincerely, many thanks! I daresay there have been repercussions of your reception here; but I have been so deep in work this last month that I haven't heard any. Tell me your news, when you get time. The Museum of Modern Art is going to hold an Architectural Show & Philip Johnson, the young man who is organizing it, would like you to be adequately represented in it. He is a side-kick of H R Hitchcock's, and, among other things, still very young: but I think it would be worth while to give him your attention. He will come west to talk things over with you, I think, if you feel this is necessary. Please consider this an introduction! Sophie joins me in warm greetings to you & Mrs Wright.

Warmly

Lewis

P.S. Why did no one ever tell me about L. Sullivan's Cedar Rapids Bank. It seems on paper the best of his later works.

P.P.S. Which tomb of his do you like best; you once said; but I don't remember.

courtesy Estate of Lewis Mumford

Frank Lloyd Wright & Lewis Mumford

THIRTY YEARS OF CORRESPONDENCE

Bruce Brooks Pfeiffer

and Robert Wojtowicz, Editors

Princeton Architectural Press

NEW YORK

Published by
Princeton Architectural Press
37 East Seventh Street
New York, New York 10003
For a free catalog of books, call 1.800.722.6657.
Visit our web site at www.papress.com.

Printed and bound in the United States
04 03 02 01 5 4 3 2 1 First edition

Project editor: Clare Jacobson
Index: Martin Jezer
Book design: Jonathan Lippincott
Cover design: Deb Wood

Special thanks to: Nettie Aljian, Ann Alter, Amanda Atkins, Nicola Bednarek, Janet Behning, Megan Carey, Penny Chu, Jan Cigliano, Jane Garvie, Tom Hutten, Mark Lamster, Nancy Eklund Later, Linda Lee, Anne Nitschke, Lottchen Shivers, and Jennifer Thompson of Princeton Architectural Press —Kevin C. Lippert, publisher

Library of Congress Cataloging-in-Publication Data
Wright, Frank Lloyd, 1867–1959.
[Correspondence. Selections]
Frank Lloyd Wright & Lewis Mumford : thirty years of correspondence / Bruce Brooks Pfeiffer and Robert Wojtowicz, editors.
p. cm.
Includes bibliographical references and index.
ISBN 1-56898-291-7 (alk. paper)
1. Wright, Frank Lloyd, 1867–1959—Correspondence. 2. Mumford, Lewis, 1895– — Correspondence. 3. Architects—United States—Correspondence. I. Title: Frank Lloyd Wright and Lewis Mumford. II. Mumford, Lewis, 1895– III. Pfeiffer, Bruce Brooks. IV. Wojtowicz, Robert. V. Title.
NA737.W7 A3 2001
720'.92–dc21

2001003808

Table of Contents

To the memory of Olgivanna Lloyd Wright and Sophia Wittenberg Mumford—partners in the correspondence

Acknowledgments

Editing a book of letters is a painstaking process whose chief reward lies in bringing long-deceased correspondents back to life on the printed page. Frank Lloyd Wright and Lewis Mumford, the protagonists of this study, were prolific letter writers who also valued the words of their counterparts. We are grateful to them for having the foresight to preserve this fascinating record of their friendship.

Without the generosity, cooperation, and permission of the Frank Lloyd Wright Foundation and the Estate of Lewis and Sophia Mumford, this study would not have been possible. We would especially like to thank Indira Berndtson, Penny Fowler, Geronimo, and Oskär Muñoz of the Wright Foundation and Elizabeth Morss, executor of the Mumford Estate. Robert Shepard, our good friend and literary agent, handled the complicated requirements of the Wright Foundation and the Mumford Estate with dispatch. Clare Jacobson of Princeton Architectural Press guided this project to completion with her usual good judgment and deliberation. Christopher Gray of Metropolitan History in New York, Terence Riley of the Museum of Modern Art in New York, Kurt G. F. Helfrich of the University of California at Santa Barbara, and Jennifer Baldwin, Julia Moore Converse, Mark Lloyd, Nancy Shawcross, and

Laura Stroffolino of the University of Pennsylvania provided essential information at very short notice. Margo Stipe of the Frank Lloyd Wright Archives graciously provided her expertise on the editing of the letters and the introduction. Madeline A. Hanlon assisted with proofreading. The accuracy of the letters' annotations is due largely to the diligence of Clay Vaughan of the Hofheimer Art Library at Old Dominion University.

Bruce Brooks Pfeiffer
Taliesin West
Scottsdale, Arizona

Robert Wojtowicz
Old Dominion University
Norfolk, Virginia

Frank Lloyd Wright
& Lewis Mumford

Introduction

BY BRUCE BROOKS PFEIFFER

AND ROBERT WOJTOWICZ

When Frank Lloyd Wright sent his first letter to Lewis Mumford in August 1926, the former was a world-renowned architect in mid-career, plagued by a series of personal and financial setbacks, while the latter was an on-the-rise cultural critic, eager to stake out a wide intellectual terrain. Despite the great difference in their ages—Wright was fifty-nine and Mumford thirty—the two formed a fast personal and creative bond within a relatively short time. Their correspondence over the next thirty-two years, which is the focus of this collection, provides a fascinating view of their respective lives and works as well as the personalities and politics that defined modern architecture in America. For if Wright (1867–1959) is generally acknowledged to be the greatest American architect of the twentieth century, then Mumford (1895–1990) was his ablest and most perceptive critic.

For Mumford, Wright's work occupied a central position in modern architecture: collectively, it was the exemplar of organic design, built in accordance with the rhythms of modern life. For Wright, Mumford's criticism was a double-edged sword. When positive, it validated the architect's often lonely creative path at a time when it seemed most of his peers were conforming to the monolithic International Style. When negative, it resurrected Wright's most profound creative insecurities, resulting in a series of hostile backlashes that only Mumford's most tactful overtures were able to overcome. Although the two men could be judged friends, they were not intimates. Wright craved a closer friendship, but Mumford steadfastly resisted it, knowing that a critic must keep his distance from his subject if his evaluations are to ring true.

The Wright–Mumford correspondence survives almost wholly intact, and as such it provides a remarkably clear window into their tumultuous relationship. Since the two men lived at a great geographical distance from one another, face-to-face encounters were infrequent. Wright alternated between Taliesin, his sprawling residential compound in Spring Green, Wisconsin and, later, Taliesin West in Scottsdale, Arizona; Mumford lived in New York City, and later in upstate Amenia, New York. Their rare meetings were most often conducted over lunch or dinner at New York's Plaza Hotel, where Wright preferred to stay while visiting the East Coast. Contact between the two was thus largely undertaken via pen and paper or telegram at a time when long-distance telephone calls were a rarity. That both men were accomplished writers—with very different epistolary styles—makes the reading of their letters all the more enjoyable and enlightening.

Frank Lloyd Wright was born to William Carey Wright and Anna Lloyd Wright in Richland Center, Wisconsin, on June 8, 1867.[1] His father was a musician and preacher; his mother, of Welsh lineage, was devoted to education and the Unitarian and transcendentalist views of Ralph Waldo Emerson and Henry David Thoreau. Anna Lloyd Wright was the dominant influence on her son, and she was convinced that he would grow up to build beautiful buildings. This strong familial background, set against the rolling, agrarian landscape of southern Wisconsin, would sustain him spiritually throughout his long life. Frank Lloyd Wright studied engineering for two semesters in 1886 at the University of Wisconsin in Madison, but left the next year for Chicago, where he entered the employ of architect Joseph Lyman Silsbee. In 1888, he joined Adler & Sullivan, one of the city's most prominent architectural firms, where he became a star draftsman. He married Catherine Lee Tobin in 1889, and the couple raised six children together in a house that the architect designed in the Chicago suburb of

Oak Park. Friction with Sullivan led Wright to establish his own architectural practice in 1893.

Wright's approach to design was revolutionary. He discarded the Romantic conventions prevalent at the turn of the twentieth century in favor of an architecture that reflected modern living. Wright termed his approach to design "organic," since it evolved naturally out of functional necessity rather than through the application of a predetermined form.[2] Building on the Arts and Crafts movement's respect for natural materials and predilection for informal living spaces, Wright designed a series of suburban houses between 1893 and 1910 that embodied the so-called "prairie style." As demonstrated in the Frederick C. Robie Residence in Chicago (1908), these were characterized by low, horizontal profiles, free-flowing interior spaces, and, when possible, the integration of the surrounding landscape with the house. His nonresidential commissions, such as the Larkin Building in Buffalo, New York (1902–1906), gave monumental expression to the rapidly changing American workplace. In the design of Unity Temple in Oak Park (1905–1908), he experimented boldly with reinforced concrete, exploring both its structural and decorative potential at a time when most architects covered this material with stone or brick.

Although Wright's practice was successful, by 1909 he was emotionally and creatively exhausted. Unhappy both in work and at home, he effectively closed his studio, abandoned his wife and children, and traveled to Europe. There he prepared material for publication in a German monograph of his work, the *Ausgeführte Bauten und Entwürfe von Frank Lloyd Wright* (1910), more commonly known as the Wasmuth Portfolio, a two-volume elephant folio filled with crisp plans and perspective views.[3] It was widely read and studied, particularly in Holland and Germany, where it had a profound effect on the development of modern architecture. Wright's romantic companion on his European journey was Mamah Borthwick Cheney, the wife of a former client. Upon the couple's return to the United States in 1911, they moved to Spring Green, Wisconsin in order to escape the disapproval of his former friends and acquaintances while he waited for his divorce. Wright began building "Taliesin" (Welsh for "shining brow")—a new home and studio that was symbolically nestled in his ancestral valley. Major commissions for the Imperial Hotel in Tokyo, Japan (1913–1922) and the Midway Gardens in Chicago (1913–1914) helped to restart Wright's practice.

Whatever economic security and personal peace Wright may have found at Taliesin was abruptly shattered in August 1914, when seven people, including Cheney and her two children, were brutally murdered and the living quarters of Taliesin set ablaze by a disgruntled servant. Overwhelmed by despair, Wright sought to mitigate his grief by rebuilding the compound. He was soon joined by Miriam Noel, a sympathetic stranger who had written to him shortly after Cheney's death. They married but they eventually separated due to Miriam Wright's emotional instability and drug addiction.

The construction of the Imperial Hotel consumed much of Wright's attention between 1916 and 1922, requiring several trips abroad. Upon his final return from Japan, Wright established himself for a time in Los Angeles, where he designed and built houses out of a novel concrete block system. The next ten years were architecturally creative if financially lean. Wright continued to experiment, turning out numerous innovative but unrealized designs. He also began writing essays for a variety of journals, most notably the polemical series titled "In the Cause of Architecture" for *Architectural Record* in 1927–1928.

Wright's reputation had soared internationally in the years following the publication of the Wasmuth Portfolio and the completion of the Imperial Hotel, drawing such prominent architects to Taliesin as Erich Mendelsohn from Germany, Werner Moser from Switzerland, Richard Neutra and Rudolph Schindler from Austria, and Kameki and Nobu Tsuchiura from Japan. Nevertheless, with no continuing work, Wright's financial worries mounted as his second marriage disintegrated. A chance encounter in late 1924 in a Chicago theater with Olgivanna Lazovich Hinzenberg, an aristocratic Eastern European émigré, thirty years Wright's junior, proved fateful. The two fell in love, and despite the fact that both were still married, Olgivanna and her daughter Svetlana moved into Taliesin in early 1925. A daughter, Iovanna, was born to the couple at the end of that year, and the ensuing public scandal lasted for several years. Adding to their difficulties, the living quarters of Taliesin once again caught fire, and, before they could be fully rebuilt, the bank took legal possession. With characteristic ingenuity, Wright decided to incorporate himself, selling shares to his friends and clients. The money he raised, however, was not enough to make the mortgage payment on Taliesin, and the bank took over the estate, evicting Wright and his new family in January 1928. It was in the midst of these myriad troubles that

Wright first contacted Lewis Mumford, who seemed to be the one critic in America sympathetic to his work.

Wright was one of a series of older influential men in Mumford's formative years and early career. Born out of wedlock in 1895, Mumford was raised by his mother on the Upper West Side of Manhattan.[4] The absence of Mumford's father was in some ways mitigated by the presence in the household of his stepgrandfather, Charles Graessel. A retired headwaiter, Graessel led Mumford on walks around the city at a time of its intense growth, awakening the young boy's interest in architecture and urbanism. Following his graduation from Stuyvesant High School in 1912, he spent several years at the City College of New York, initially in the evening session and subsequently as a daytime student. A diagnosis of incipient tuberculosis forced his withdrawal in 1914, but even before this his autodidactic temperament led him to rebel against the rigidity of the college's curriculum. Like Wright, Mumford never earned his baccalaureate degree, and he remained a strong critic of the academy throughout his life.

While still a student, Mumford happened across the writings of Patrick Geddes, the Scottish polymath who proposed an evolutionary and regional approach to the study of modern society. In emulation of Geddes, Mumford began surveying the New York metropolitan area by train, ferry, and foot, noting everything from geological outcroppings to jerrybuilt residential subdivisions. Cities—as gathering places for people, ideas, buildings, and cultural activities—began to emerge as his focus. Mumford and Geddes began corresponding in 1917, but when the two first met in 1923, it became apparent that Geddes was seeking a collaborator who would carry on his life's work. Mumford backed away, determined that his own career take precedence.[5]

The ideas of Ebenezer Howard also exerted a profound influence on Mumford at this stage. Not long after first encountering Geddes's ideas, Mumford read Howard's *Garden Cities of To-morrow* (1902), a radical utopian tract that advocated the planting of self-sufficient communities of moderate size on the outskirts of major British cities, but separated physically by agricultural greenbelts.[6] Howard's garden cities ideally would combine the best advantages of urban and rural living without degenerating into the amorphous suburbs already engulfing London and other major cities. Over the next several decades, Mumford became the chief advocate for the garden city in the United States.

Mumford's departure from City College freed him to pursue his varied intellectual interests while attempting to launch a career as a journalist. He was inducted into the U.S. Navy near the end of World War I, but he remained stateside and resolutely continued to write while off-duty. Not long after he was discharged in early 1919, his work began to appear in a variety of publications, including the *Dial*, *Sociological Review*, *Freeman*, *Journal of the American Institute of Architects*, *New Republic*, and, after 1931, *New Yorker*. His versatility as a critic was astonishing; he wrote pieces on topics as diverse as art, architecture, literature, theater, sociology, and politics.

Architecture, however, emerged as Mumford's strongest metier as he began to question the suitability of then-popular Romantic revivalism to the exigencies of modern life. His early, appreciative reading of Claude Bragdon's *Architecture and Democracy* (1918), which espoused an organic approach to modern design, is especially notable in this regard.[7] Personal and professional success came quickly. In 1921, Mumford married Sophia Wittenberg, a former colleague at the *Dial*, who became his closest intellectual compatriot and life-long amanuensis. The following year, Mumford published his first book, *The Story of Utopias* (1922), a survey of utopian literature that ended with a call for regional surveying and the re-planning of the American landscape utilizing garden cities.[8]

In 1923, Mumford joined the Regional Planning Association of America, a loosely organized group of architects, planners, economists, and writers who embraced Geddes's regionalism and Howard's garden city model as a two-pronged solution to the metropolitan sprawl overtaking the East Coast of the United States.[9] Over the next decade, the association effectively combined Geddes's and Howard's ideas to form the "regional city," a self-contained community that was of moderate density yet closely balanced with its rural surroundings. As secretary, Mumford acted as the group's principal spokesperson, publicizing their ideas and projects in a variety of journals.

The Regional Planning Association of America is best known for conceiving the Appalachian Trail, but it also developed two influential residential communities in the New York metropolitan area. The first, Sunnyside Gardens in Long Island City, Queens (1924–1928), is a neighborhood of small townhouses and apartments built around common green interior courts. Lewis and Sophia Mumford moved to Sunnyside Gardens in 1925 following the birth of their son Geddes—named for Mumford's mentor—and remained there until just after the birth of their daughter Alison in 1936, when they relocated permanently to a farmhouse in upstate Dutchess County, New York. The second, Radburn in Bergen County, New Jersey (1928–1932), was far more ambitious. Conceived as a regional city, it was eventually scaled back to a garden suburb. Unfortunately, the Depression bankrupted the project, and drove the association's members to disband by the early 1930s.

Mumford's principal focus during the 1920s remained his writing, however. On the advice of Van Wyck Brooks, an older literary critic and close friend, Mumford spent several years uncovering America's "usable past"[10]—the rich but largely hidden creative output of the nineteenth century. In his next four books, Mumford reasoned that the historian might "use" this rediscovered past to impel his contemporaries to greater achievements. *Sticks and Stones* (1924), the first book to emerge from this investigation, was a survey of American architecture that eschewed the usual organizing rubric of style, instead positing a social analysis of buildings' forms and functions.[11] The controversy this book generated, especially among the conservative followers of the French Ecole des Beaux-Arts, branded Mumford as an iconoclastic critic. The book's translation into German the following year, moreover, brought Mumford's views to the attention of such European modernists as Walter Gropius, Ernst May, and Erich Mendelsohn.[12]

Mumford's next book, *The Golden Day* (1926), surveyed American literature with particular emphasis on Ralph Waldo Emerson, Henry David Thoreau, Nathaniel Hawthorne, Herman Melville, and Walt Whitman, an esteemed group of writers whose works drew inspiration freely from the American landscape.[13] *Herman Melville* (1929) was a full-length, psychologically penetrating biography of the enigmatic author.[14] In *The Brown Decades* (1931), the last of these early books, Mumford concentrated on what he identified as a creative efflorescence in all of the arts of the late nineteenth century.[15]

Wright entered Mumford's life midway through the "usable past" project; what had been Mumford's abstract analysis of the past suddenly became a living engagement with it. The timing could not have been more fortuitous. Before the mid-1920s, Mumford had not traveled much beyond the northeastern United States, and he was aware of Wright's architecture only through photographs, publications, and the eyewitness accounts of colleagues such as Mendelsohn. For this reason, Mumford mentioned Wright only in passing in *Sticks and Stones*.[16] Any mention at all, however, was important to Wright at this troubled point in his career.

In 1925, Hendricus Wijdeveld, editor of the Dutch journal *Wendingen*, dedicated a special issue to Wright and invited Mumford to contribute an essay.[17] Although Mumford later deemed his essay "pathetically meager and tentative,"[18] in it he established three themes that were to recur in his criticism. First, he identified Wright as continuing a line of creative innovation that had been initiated by H. H. Richardson and Louis Sullivan in the late nineteenth century and that had been nearly obliterated by the resurgent Romantic revivalism of the early twentieth century. Second, Mumford placed Wright in opposition to the machine-like functionalism of emerging European modernists such as Le Corbusier. Third, Mumford saw in Wright's work an ideal modern synthesis of function and expression that was at the same time in harmony with the American landscape. Mumford went so far as to compare Wright's architecture to Carl Sandburg's poetry and Sherwood Anderson's novels for their uniquely mid-American qualities.[19]

Mumford reiterated many of these ideas in another article, "The Poison of Good Taste," for *The American Mercury*.[20] It was this piece that prompted Wright's initial communication to Mumford in August 1926, in which he lamented the *Wendingen* "obituaries" and questioned the depths of Mumford's understanding of his architecture.[21] Mumford's apology completed the exchange later that month,[22] but it was not until the winter of 1926–1927 that the two men first met and their friendship was launched. With affection, Mumford recounted this first luncheon meeting at the Plaza Hotel in his autobiography:

> Wright and I were never more friendly and at ease than we were at that first exploratory luncheon; he was disarmingly candid: almost painfully so, as sometimes happens more easily with a stranger than with an old friend or future associate. He confessed at the beginning that he was financially broke; indeed he had come to New York to find someone who would pur-

> chase his collection of Japanese prints, so as to stave off his ever-threatening creditors. . . .
>
> None of the tragedies of his life, none of the harassing episodes that had followed, had corroded his spirit or sapped his energies: his face was unseamed, his air assured, indeed jaunty. Was he, then, lacking in sensitiveness or sensibility? Yes and no! More probably, I am driven to believe, his ego was so heavily armored that even the bursting shell of such disastrous events did not penetrate his vital organs. He lived from first to last like a God: one who acts but is not acted upon.[23]

The Wright–Mumford friendship was rooted firmly on a shared appreciation of the American landscape and a special admiration for the transcendentalist writings of Emerson and Thoreau. From reading Claude Bragdon, Mumford had already come to embrace the construct of an organic modern architecture of which Wright was the leading theorist and practitioner. Furthermore, both Wright and Mumford disliked skyscrapers and metropolitan congestion, but whereas the former would call for the elimination of the traditional city, the latter would advocate for its rebuilding using the regional city as a model. Yet, even at their first meeting, the sheer force of Wright's personality must have caused Mumford some concern. Already Mumford had refused Patrick Geddes's earnest invitation of an assistantship, and he was not about to yield his independence as a critic to another.

Almost immediately after their meeting, Mumford embarked on a lecture tour of the Midwest that finally brought him into direct contact with Wright's architecture in Chicago and its suburbs. Wright and Mumford did not connect on this trip, but one of Mumford's guides was Barry Byrne, an architect who had once worked for Wright at the Oak Park Studio. Mumford summarized his findings in a November 1927 article in which he identified "a great school" of architects at work in late-nineteenth-century Chicago.[24] In Mumford's view, Wright held a special position within this group since his work was both the culmination of a progressive lineage that had begun in the 1880s with Richardson, Sullivan, and John Wellborn Root, and a contemporary bridge to European modernism. "There is no Eastern architect upon whom European attention is so firmly centered as upon Mr. Frank Lloyd Wright," Mumford wrote. "There is no other American architect in our history who has had such a deep influence outside his own country."[25]

Letters between Wright and Mumford became more frequent, beginning in spring 1928. As the elder correspondent, Wright tended to dominate the exchange. Topics covered ranged from his treatment at the hands of other historians and critics—most notably Fiske Kimball, Henry-Russell Hitchcock, Jr., and Douglas Haskell—to his various architectural, educational, and writing projects. Mumford began to write with confidence of his own work, particularly his biography-in-progress of Herman Melville.

As they gradually became more familiar, they broached personal subjects: Wright's marriage to Olgivanna Lazovich in August 1928, delayed by his divorce from Miriam Wright, and four-year-old Geddes Mumford's near-fatal mastoid infection the following spring. Wright wrote several teasing references to Catherine Bauer, a latecomer to the Regional Planning Association of America, with whom Mumford became romantically involved for several years. The two men also exchanged photographs and other printed materials. Yet, on more than one occasion, when Wright invited Mumford and his family to visit Taliesin, the critic demurred, citing the ongoing pressures of free-lance writing. "Wright could not understand my unwillingness to abandon my vocation as a writer to have the honor of serving his genius," Mumford wrote in his autobiography, "and he was puzzled, almost nettled, over my unreadiness to break into my own work at any given moment to be his guest."[26] Mumford's refusal established a pattern of missed opportunities that lasted for the duration of their friendship.

Wright only made oblique references to his personal and financial woes in his early letters to Mumford, and in 1927 the architect's fortunes actually seemed to be improving. Wright received an offer to consult with architect Albert Chase McArthur on the design of the Arizona Biltmore Hotel in Phoenix. Shortly after he arrived in Phoenix, he was hired by Dr. Alexander Chandler to build a new resort hotel in the desert on the outskirts of the city. Rather than rent space, Wright elected to build a work camp for his family and his newly assembled staff. He named it "Ocotilla" after a native desert cactus. Wright found life in the desert, though decidedly primitive, to be richly invigorating. At about this time, he also received a commission to design a high-rise apartment building in New York City, St. Mark's-in-the-Bouwerie. The stock market crash of October 1929, however, brought all of Wright's projects to an abrupt halt.

With little architectural work on hand, Wright turned to lecturing and writing his autobiography. In May 1930 he delivered the Kahn Lectures at Princeton University to enthusiastic audiences. These were subsequently published as *Modern Architecture*.[27] He also prepared a large exhibition of his work that toured several cities in the United States, Holland, Belgium, and Germany. *An Autobiography* was published in March 1932 to general critical acclaim, including Mumford's favorable notice.[28] "Mr. Wright's book is a literary act that compares in brilliance and originality with his buildings," Mumford wrote, "a work with the marks of a novelist, indeed of a poet, on almost every page."[29] That same year, Wright published *The Disappearing City*, which argued for the radical decentralization of the nation's cities, a position on which he and Mumford disagreed profoundly.[30]

Mumford was, in the meantime, finishing work on the "usable past" project. Ever since visiting Chicago in 1927, he had been determined to correct the cursory treatment he had given late-nineteenth-century American architecture in *Sticks and Stones*. Wright was, in fact, among those colleagues who urged Mumford to undertake a new architectural study, but Mumford did not begin serious work on it until he completed his Melville biography in 1929.[31] By summer 1930, Mumford was deep into the writing of *The Brown Decades*. Confident of his developing friendship with Wright, he peppered the architect on two separate occasions with questions about his work and about the influence of Louis Sullivan.[32] Wright's lengthy responses reveal a great deal about his relationship with Sullivan, his approach to ornament, and his personal estimation of selected buildings.[33] As additional background information, Wright sent Mumford a carbon copy of the Princeton lectures he had delivered the previous spring.

Mumford was at this point stepping into uncharted territory from a critical standpoint. Since Wright was both a historical figure and a living contemporary, any information derived from him would necessarily be subjective. By happenstance, George Elmslie, a former colleague of Wright at the Oak Park Studio who had also worked under Sullivan, contacted Mumford after reading an early published draft of the book's architecture chapter in spring 1931.[34] Their exchange of letters allowed

Mumford to clarify many of his arguments, particularly concerning Sullivan's key position in the so-called "Chicago school."

Published in 1931, *The Brown Decades* culminated Mumford's "usable past" project by reassessing all of the arts of late-nineteenth-century America. While *The Golden Day* established a pantheon of writers, *The Brown Decades* added notable figures in other creative fields: Richardson, Root, and Sullivan in architecture; John and Washington Roebling in engineering; Frederick Law Olmsted in landscape architecture; and Thomas Eakins and Alfred Pinkham Ryder in painting. Mumford further identified the photographer Alfred Stieglitz and Wright as artists with creative roots in this period who, nevertheless, remained two of the most vital forces on the contemporary scene. In particular, Mumford admired Wright's subordination of the mechanical or the "technic"—an arcane term that the critic increasingly favored—to modern human needs. Mumford wrote:

> His architecture, though he has pioneered with modern methods of construction and delighted in mechanical techniques, is not merely a passive adaptation to the machine age: it is a reaching toward a more biotechnic economy, better grounded in the permanent realities of birth, growth, reproduction, and the natural environment than is the dominant order of paper values and merely mechanical efficiencies.[35]

Although Mumford's treatment of Wright was generally favorable—even adulatory in certain passages—the critic identified "one great weakness" in the architect's individualistic and comprehensive approach to design:

> A man of genius delights in such a load: but architecture as a social art cannot depend upon the existence of men of genius: when it is in a healthy state it relies upon the commonplace effects of the carpenter, the builder, the engineer, the manufacturer, and the task of the architect is not to usurp the work that is done in these departments, but to organize it intelligently and to create out of it an orderly composition.[36]

On that one point alone, Wright's response to *The Brown Decades* was understandably tepid.[37] Moreover, as a practicing architect, Wright did not like being treated as a historical figure. He was especially irked by Mumford's discussion of the "lineage" of American architecture, since it suggested a false line of succession. Although devoted to his *lieber Meister*, Louis Sullivan, Wright emphatically maintained that he was Sullivan's "pupil," not his "disciple."[38] Nevertheless, Mumford had become too valuable an ally at this point in Wright's career to risk overt disagreement.

Two major architectural controversies involving Mumford and Wright bracketed the publication of *The Brown Decades*. The first centered upon Wright's exclusion from the 1933 World's Fair in Chicago, otherwise known as the Century of Progress Exposition. Architect Raymond Hood, who served as co-nominator on the fair's architectural commission, arbitrarily made the decision to bar Wright because of his perceived inability to work with others. Mumford leapt to Wright's defense in a January 1931 piece for the *New Republic*:

> The omission of Frank Lloyd Wright is serious. It is also very funny. As the years go on the joke will seem funnier and funnier. "Hamlet" without the Prince of Denmark could not be a more comical performance. Perhaps the largest claim that the distinguished architects now in charge of the Fair will have on the attention of posterity will be through this little omission.[39]

Wright and Hood exchanged heated letters the following month, and Wright copied Mumford so as to provide the critic with potential ammunition for a public forum on the matter sponsored by the American Union of Decorative Artists and Craftsmen in New York City's Town Hall that March. Wright recounted the "packed" meeting in his autobiography:

> At once the meeting took on an air of laughing gaiety. But that changed when Lewis Mumford got up to speak. With the essential manliness and nobility seen in the man as seen in his work he made no attempt to be apologetic or conciliatory. He was earnest and seriously wrote down the matter of the Fair where modern architecture was concerned more clearly and effectively than I had done the evening before.[40]

Despite this show of support by Mumford and others, Wright remained on the fair's sidelines.

The second controversy surrounded the *Modern Architecture: International Exhibition* held at the Museum of Modern Art in New York in 1932 and co-curated by Henry-Russell Hitchcock, Jr. and

Philip Johnson.[41] As a critic who disavowed the importance of style and who advocated a regional basis for modern architectural expression, Mumford was skeptical of the museum's intent to define an emerging International Style. Furthermore, the proposed exhibition's emphasis on European architecture and machine aesthetics also troubled him. Mumford and Hitchcock had been corresponding for several years, and the two disagreed over Hitchcock's identification and promotion of a select group of progressive European architects that he labeled the "New Pioneers." This group, which included Gropius, Ludwig Mies van der Rohe, J. J. P. Oud, and Le Corbusier, was to form the nucleus of the exhibition. Nevertheless, Mumford saw great merit in the Europeans' stripped-down forms—so unlike the ornament-encrusted Art Deco and Romantic-revival buildings of contemporary American practice—and also in their coordinated, government-sponsored approach to solving the post–World War I housing crisis. Wright's placement in the exhibition posed a particular problem for Hitchcock and Johnson—and indirectly, as it turned out, for Mumford. To ignore Wright would have left a gaping hole in the already weak "American" section, but neither curator was willing to rank him with the "New Pioneers."

In January 1931, Johnson invited Mumford to participate in the housing section of the exhibition. Mumford was well-prepared for this task because of his experience with the Regional Planning Association of America, but also because of his knowledge of recent European housing initiatives acquired largely through Catherine Bauer. (Bauer had visited many of the European housing developments, or *Siedlungen*, and gave Mumford a first-hand account of their successes and flaws.) This limited role was to have been Mumford's sole contribution, but, quite unexpectedly, Mumford found himself acting as mediator between the curators and Wright. Wright did not know Johnson at this point, but Wright and Hitchcock had for some time been at odds over Hitchcock's various published appraisals of the architect's work.

Mumford relayed news of the exhibition to Wright in March 1931, along with an introduction to Johnson.[42] Subsequently, Johnson wrote the architect, asking him to take part in the show.[43] Wright was predictably unenthusiastic about his proposed inclusion with the Europeans, but he accepted the museum's invitation somewhat reluctantly and later that year began work on his House on the Mesa project.

Wright remained wary of the exhibition as it developed over the next several months, especially the prominence being given to Le Corbusier. The Europeans, he believed, designed more like painters than architects, working in two dimensions rather than three.

The situation came to a head in January 1932, when Wright threatened to pull out of the exhibition after he learned of the inclusion of Raymond Hood and Richard Neutra.[44] In general Wright disliked Hood's stylistic eclecticism, but the case with Neutra was far more personal. Neutra had worked for Wright in the mid-1920s, soon after immigrating to the United States. According to Wright, Neutra falsely promoted himself, using his connections with his former employer to advance his own career. Wright proposed mounting his own exhibition, but Mumford telegraphed the architect immediately, urging him to reconsider.[45] Wright relented, telegraphing his response to Mumford the very same day.[46] He contributed a model of the House on the Mesa to the exhibition; its bold geometry effectively put to rest the curators' contention that he was a nineteenth-century architect.

When the show opened in early February, Mumford wrote to Wright and explained his position on the International Style and, in particular, the communitarian—verging on communistic—aspects of modern housing, which he had emphasized in his own essay for the exhibition's catalog.[47] Later that month, Mumford reviewed the exhibition for the *New Yorker* in his new role as the magazine's architecture critic.[48] Calling the show "a great triumph for Frank Lloyd Wright," Mumford argued that the architect's work compared very favorably with its European counterparts:

> Mr. Wright's work is not so far away from the best European architecture as he imagines—or as they perhaps do. His new buildings have lost the ornamental exuberance of the Midway Gardens and the Imperial Hotel: they are more in the line of his earlier houses. Meanwhile, the Europeans have moved nearer to Wright: passing from dogma to building, they have lost a little of their faith in ferro-concrete as an absolute; they have acquired some of Wright's love for natural materials, his interest in the site and the landscape, his feeling for the region.[49]

That summer, Mumford finally visited many of the European *Siedlungen* in the company of Catherine Bauer. Mumford reported to Wright that while the housing was generally good, the architecture represented in the International Style show "in reality is not as brave in fact as it seems in literature."[50]

In October 1932, Wright and Olgivanna welcomed twenty-three young men and women at Taliesin to enroll in a new school they called the Taliesin Fellowship. The fellowship was to be an experiential apprenticeship program for young architects who would work in Wright's studio as well as construct projects and farm on the estate. The tuition generated by the fellowship enabled Wright to improve his financial situation and revive his practice. Wright asked Hendricus Wijdeveld to lead the school, but after spending time together in late 1931, Wright concluded that "Dutchy" was "too much of a lyrical egoist" to be more than a participating faculty member.[51] In February 1932, at the height of the International Style controversy, Wright extended the same invitation to Mumford.[52] Although Mumford had already assumed occasional teaching duties, most notably at Dartmouth College (1929–1935), he declined Wright's invitation, this time citing his current book in progress.[53] The fellowship was launched without Mumford's participation.

In late 1934, Wright and his apprentices began construction on a large-scale wooden model of Broadacre City, a project for decentralizing America's urban centers that he had first articulated in *The Disappearing City*. According to Wright's vision, a series of low-density Broadacre communities would be discreetly zoned for residential, commercial, industrial, and agricultural use and linked via automobile or the autogiro, an experimental form of the helicopter. Freestanding houses of various sizes for people of varying income levels were to be placed on a minimum of an acre of land. The model was completed in Arizona, where Wright moved temporarily with the fellowship in January 1935 to escape the cold Wisconsin winter.

That spring the model toured several major cities, including New York, where it was exhibited at the Industrial Arts Exposition at Rockefeller Center. "Broadacre City, as Wright has conceived it, is both a generous dream and a rational plan," Mumford wrote in his review for the *New Yorker*, "and in both respects it adds valuable elements that have been left out of a great many current projects for the replanning of our cities and countrysides."[54] Yet Mumford, whose experience with the

Regional Planning Association of America had convinced him that terrace-block housing surrounding communal spaces worked best in modest residential neighborhoods, questioned Wright's design:

> The weakest point in Broadacre City is the design of the minimal house. Wright, who hates the very word "housing," has created a design for single-family houses for the lower-income groups which compares very unfavorably, I think, with the European and American "housing" he detests. He should have permitted himself to dream more generously. As soon as he reaches the level of the "two-car" house, he shows that he is still our most original architect, as capable of producing beauty in standardized units as in his favored materials that spring out of the earth.[55]

The somewhat heated exchange of letters that followed Mumford's review reveals how divergent their attitudes toward cities truly were. Wright stubbornly refused to see any value in what he termed "the German tenement and slum solution," while Mumford, despite his bias toward garden cities, conceived of a variety of potential forms for new, medium-density communities, ranging from Sunnyside Gardens and the European *Siedlungen* to Broadacre City.[56] Far more influential than Broadacre City were Wright's related designs for low-cost, one-story "Usonian" houses. These caught the attention of a new generation of middle-class suburban homebuyers, eager to spread out over the American landscape.

In the mid-1930s, Wright received several major commissions that effectively tested the limits of reinforced concrete engineering, while bringing him national and international acclaim. These included the Edgar J. Kaufmann Residence in southwestern Pennsylvania (1935), more popularly known as "Fallingwater," and the S. C. Johnson & Son Headquarters Building in Racine, Wisconsin (1936). With these two projects alone, Wright's placement as the greatest American architect of the twentieth century, if not of all time, was irrevocably secured. Mumford did not travel to either place, although he did see a photographic exhibition of the Kaufmann House at the Museum of Modern Art in 1938. Mumford reviewed the exhibition glowingly in the *New Yorker*:

> Whether it was Wright or his client who thought of building a house over a waterfall I do not know, but Wright's imagination played with the

> opportunity as freely as Michelangelo's played with the decoration of the Sistine Chapel. The perpetual youngness and freshness of his mind were never better shown than in his treatment of this extraordinary problem. The site would have frightened any conventional architect out of his wits. Wright uses the opportunity to demonstrate that when the need arises he can swing a cantilever across space, using the method of construction not as a cliché of modernism but as a rational engineering solution of a real problem.[57]

With his notoriety reestablished and on the advice of a doctor, Wright decided to make Arizona his permanent winter home. In December 1937, he and Olgivanna scouted the area around Phoenix for property and decided upon a site at the foot of the McDowell Mountains northeast of the city. The fellowship set up a temporary camp adjacent to the construction site, and the Wrights occupied a tent nearby. If life in Ocotilla eight years earlier seemed primitive, this new life on the desert was even more so as "Taliesin West" took shape. The compound eventually grew to more than a half-dozen buildings surrounded by 600 acres.

Interest in Wright and the fellowship grew steadily. In January 1938, the *Architectural Forum* devoted its entire issue to him, and that same month, Wright appeared on the cover of *Time*.[58] A series of lectures Wright gave in London in spring 1939 were published as *An Organic Architecture*.[59] During 1939 alone, Wright received forty new commissions, a welcome and gratifying resurgence. To protect his work, drawings, and legacy, Wright established the nonprofit Frank Lloyd Wright Foundation in 1940. The Museum of Modern Art in New York held a large exhibition of his work in winter 1940–1941, which was to some degree documented in Henry-Russell Hitchcock, Jr.'s *In the Nature of Materials* (1942).[60] At about the same time, Frederick Gutheim edited *Frank Lloyd Wright on Architecture: Selected Writings, 1894–1940*.[61] In 1941 Wright was awarded the gold medal of the Royal Institute of British Architects.

While Wright's work and celebrity increased in the mid-to-late 1930s, his letters to and meetings with Mumford decreased. Mumford's career, like Wright's, was undergoing a major shift at this time. Even before completing the "usable past" project, he had begun moving beyond the confines of American cultural studies to the broader plain of Western civilization, where he believed his intellectual mark would be greater. The book in progress, to which he referred in his 1932 letter, eventually grew into a monumental four-volume work, The Renewal of Life series, that surveyed Western civilization from the middle ages to the twentieth century. The series drew heavily upon Patrick Geddes's ideas regarding civilization's decline during the industrial, "paleotechnic" era of the nineteenth century and its potential for renewal in the cleanly powered and regionally based "neotechnic" era of the twentieth. *Technics and Civilization* (1934), the first volume in Mumford's series, chronicled the history of technology, while the second, *The Culture of Cities* (1938) covered the history of urbanism.[62] The overriding theme of both books was the harnessing of the "technic" in the service of the "organic," which Mumford defined as the fullest realization of human potential. In *Technics and Civilization* Mumford mentioned Wright only in passing, but significantly, as an exemplar of the organic:

> So the organic approach in thought is important today because we have begun, here and there, to act on these terms even when unaware of the conceptual implications. This development has gone on in architecture from Sullivan and Frank Lloyd Wright to the new architects in Europe, and from [Robert] Owen and Ebenezer Howard and Patrick Geddes in city design to the community planners in Holland, Germany, and Switzerland who have begun to crystallize in a fresh pattern the whole neotechnic environment.[63]

Following its publication, Mumford inscribed a copy of the book to Wright, who in turn called it a "great work."[64]

Wright figured more prominently in *The Culture of Cities*, but Mumford continued his criticism of Broadacre City, calling it "an overcompensated protest against the reckless and indiscriminate congestion of the metropolis."[65] Wright's reaction to this book is unknown, but doubtless he was dismayed by Mumford's assessment. *The Culture of Cities* proved to be Mumford's most successful work to date. Reviewers were generally enthusiastic, and Mumford himself appeared on the cover of *Time* magazine three months after Wright was accorded the same honor.[66] From this point forward, he was recognized internationally as an authority on the history and planning of cities.

Since the disagreement over Broadacre City, the two men had virtually halted their correspondence. In April 1941 Mumford delivered the Dancy Lectures at Alabama College, subsequently published as *The*

South in Architecture, in which he focused on the works of Thomas Jefferson and H. H. Richardson, but also spoke appreciatively of Wright's residential architecture.[67] That same month, Mumford wrote to Wright primarily to express his outrage over the threatened demolition of the Robie House in Chicago, but also to reestablish contact and to broach the subject of politics.[68]

Since first encountering Nazism on his 1932 European journey, Mumford, himself a liberal Democrat, had been watching the political situation there anxiously. In the late 1930s, Mumford had taken a public, interventionist stand against Nazism and Fascism in numerous articles and in two books: *Men Must Act* (1939) and *Faith for Living* (1940).[69] Wright felt differently. Although his idiosyncratic political views may seem to be those of an avowed isolationist, he disclaimed the term. "Who are the great Isolationists of the world today?" he later wrote to another friend. "Churchill and Stalin, of course. Isolationist is one who goes with the world so long as it is going his way and otherwise won't go."[70] Early in 1941 Wright expressed his opposition to the United States' involvement in World War II. He wrote:

> HITLER IS WINNING THIS WAR WITHOUT A NAVY. We are facing a new kind of warfare that the British Empire, owing to traditional faith in a great navy, cannot learn in time even if we furnished the equipment.... Our frontier is no longer England nor, in any sense, is it European. Our frontier is our own shores.[71]

When Mumford received this broadside, it infuriated him. "You dishonor all the generous impulses you once ennobled," he wrote in a letter to Wright. "Be silent! lest you bring upon yourself some greater shame."[72] Wright's reply was just as vitriolic. "There is no good Empire;" he wrote, "there never was a just war."[73] Thus a fine and productive friendship came to an abrupt end. Wright remained steadfastly opposed to World War II—and all wars—until his death.

Wright was not the only friend Mumford lost because of his political beliefs, but this rift affected him deeply. As Mumford later recalled in his autobiography:

> In that crisis our friendship had come to an end; so much so that I did not open till years later the New Year's messages he continued to send me. But I smiled grimly when I received a greeting from him—sent at a time when

there was a stringent paper shortage—in an envelope eighteen inches long, containing a folded greeting on heavy paper twice the length of the envelope! During the early forties that insolent symbol seemed final.[74]

Adding further insult, Mumford published his letter to Wright in the interventionist periodical, the *New Leader*.[75] Later that fall, Wright reviewed Mumford's *The South in Architecture*. While the overall tone of the review was negative, a glimmer of the architect's lingering affection for the critic can be read between the lines. Objecting once again to Mumford's restatement of Wright's Chicago school lineage, the architect wrote:

No Lewis! While I am hardly looking, you can't bring this man Richardson up on me from behind, slip in a coupling pin, and ask me to take him along! Moreover, can't you see, Lewis, that according to your view of me you are only turning him over to the Japanese?[76]

Ten years passed before the two men communicated again. Despite this break, Mumford retained an admiration for Wright's work and an affection for the man as expressed in Mumford's 1946 letter to poet John Gould Fletcher:

I should say he is one of the great architectural geniuses of our time; not merely that, but of any time . . . He has more imagination in his little finger than most of his contemporaries have in their whole organism; and his combination of the poet and the engineer is a rare one, though the poet is sometimes capricious and [the] engineer uses his great talent to perform stunts.[77]

The war years were a very lean time for the Taliesin Fellowship. Most of Wright's apprentices had either enlisted or been drafted into the armed forces. Those who remained devoted their time to working the farm. Architectural commissions had also dropped off sharply. In 1943 Wright received a commission to design a museum to house the nonobjective painting collection of the Solomon R. Guggenheim Foundation. This commission, one of the most important and contentious of his career, would provoke a sixteen-year battle between architect, client, trustees, and the city of New York. Tragedy again struck Wright in 1946 when his daughter Svetlana died in an automobile accident along with her son Daniel and an unborn child. It was a loss from which Olgivanna Wright never fully recovered.

Once the War ended, the fellowship flourished anew, expanding to sixty apprentices from all over the world, and once again Wright's career took flight. The *Architectural Forum* devoted both its January 1948 and January 1951 issues to Wright. In March 1949 the American Institute of Architects, an organization to which Wright had never belonged—and of which he greatly disapproved—awarded him its Gold Medal. In early 1951, *Sixty Years of Living Architecture*, the largest exhibition of his work to date, opened in Philadelphia, before traveling to several European and American venues. While in Florence for the exhibition's opening, he received the de Medici medal; in Venice he received the Star of Solidarity, Italy's highest honor. In June, almost exactly ten years to the day he and Mumford had dissolved their friendship, he sent Mumford the preface to the Florence exhibition.[78]

When Wright reinitiated contact with Mumford in spring 1951, the two men were on vastly different footings. Wright at eighty-four was at the very peak of his creativity. Mumford at fifty-five was a leading authority on architecture and urbanism, but also recognized as a public intellectual who brought his moral authority to bear on a variety of contemporary political and social issues. Subsequently, the chronological gap between them seemed to narrow. Yet ironically, the very egotism that Mumford had long detested in Wright's character had by this time become integral to his own.

Mumford had been affected by numerous professional and personal changes. Although he joined the faculty of Stanford University's fledgling School of Humanities in 1942, he realized that he was not well suited to holding a full-time academic appointment. He left this position in 1944 and returned with his family to their farmhouse in upstate New York. During this time, Mumford was chiefly at work completing the last two volumes of The Renewal of Life series. Written during and immediately after World War II, *The Condition of Man* (1944) and *The Conduct of Life* (1951), the series' last two volumes, examined the history of human beliefs and values, which Mumford believed held even greater relevance in this period of crisis and rebuilding.[79] This was a period of personal crisis and rebuilding for Mumford and his family as well. In 1944, nineteen-year-old Geddes was killed in action while serving on the Allied front lines in Italy. Grief-stricken, Mumford plunged headfirst into the writing of *Green Memories* (1947), an intimate biography of his slain son that is equally revealing of his own doubts and insecurities about fatherhood and marriage.[80]

As peace gave way to the uncertainties of the Cold War, Mumford redirected his political energies toward halting the emerging nuclear arms race. The totalitarian threat he feared had passed only to be replaced by a technological determinism that held an even greater potential for disaster. Professionally, the 1950s were to be an especially productive decade for Mumford, who was at work revising *Sticks and Stones* (1955) and *The Brown Decades* (1955), editing *Roots of Contemporary American Architecture* (1952), writing *The Transformations of Man* (1956), and researching *The City in History* (1961).[81] Architectural criticism became a secondary activity for him, although he kept his column for the *New Yorker*.

Mumford had for many years resisted answering Wright's New Year's greetings, but when in spring 1951 the architect sent a copy of his exhibition catalog, *Sixty Years of Living Architecture*—inscribed "In spite of all, your old F.Ll.W."—Mumford was deeply moved. As he recalled in his autobiography:

> When I saw this, I turned to Sophia and said: "I've just written a book in which I've said that without a great upsurgence of love, we shall not be able to save the world from even greater orgies of extermination and destruction. If I haven't enough love left in me to answer Wright in the same fashion as this greeting, I'd better throw that book out the window." So I wrote him, repeating my words to Sophia; and he answered in his characteristically generous fashion by sending me an inscribed print of a winter scene by [Hiroshige].[82]

The time was ripe for reconciliation. Coincidentally, Mumford had just given a series of lectures at Columbia University that included a generous appraisal of Wright's work.[83] Once the dam was breached, words and ideas flowed anew. The language was somewhat tentative compared to their earlier correspondence, an indication of the tension still smoldering beneath the surface. Nevertheless, with great eagerness the two men planned their reunion luncheon at the Plaza Hotel in February 1952. "But it's a dozen years since we met & much has happened," Mumford warned the architect, "so don't be too shocked."[84] By both accounts, the meeting was a resounding success, with Wright busily making loose sketches of Sullivan's Wainwright Tomb in St. Louis (1890) and Walker Warehouse in Chicago (1888–1889); Mumford took these with him as souvenirs.

The letters of the first few years of this decade are filled with news of family, reports of works in progress, discussions of the International Style, and sparring over the spelling of Mumford's name—Wright preferred the Welsh-inspired, Llewis. The two exchanged books as well, including Mumford's biography of his son, which Wright tactfully acknowledged even as he restated his pacifist position.[85] Mumford convinced Wright to submit one of his early essays, "The Art and Craft of the Machine" (1901, revised 1930), to the collection *Roots of Contemporary Architecture*.[86] Olgivanna Wright and Sophia Mumford soon joined the dialogue, both as subjects and as active correspondents when their husbands were otherwise preoccupied; in their letters one glimpses the strains and joys of marriage to public figures. Several times Wright proffered invitations to Taliesin, but Mumford again declined, citing various illnesses, along with his writing and part-time academic appointments at North Carolina State University (1948–1952), the University of Pennsylvania (1951–1956, 1959–1961), and the Massachusetts Institute of Technology (1957–1961). Not surprisingly, Mumford's refusal caused Wright considerable consternation.

This last decade of Wright's life was in many ways his most triumphant. He appeared regularly on the lecture circuit, and he conquered the new broadcast medium of television. In 1953, he began an association with a new publisher, Horizon Press, and printed a new book for each of the next seven years.[87] These books included *A Testament* (1957), which was comprised largely of new material. Ground was finally broken for the long-delayed Guggenheim Museum in New York in 1956. The following year brought an avalanche of new commissions. Indeed it seemed as though Wright's energies knew no confines; he was ninety years old and more productive than he had been in any previous decade of his life.

Mumford had long considered writing an extended critical evaluation of Wright's life and work. The opportunity presented itself in 1953 when the exhibition *Sixty Years of Living Architecture* opened in a temporary pavilion on the Guggenheim's building site. Wright, in fact, led Mumford on a personal tour of the exhibition, but by Mumford's account the meeting was extraordinarily frustrating due to the architect's overwhelming egoism. "In seeing his life, so to say, spread before me, with his voice as a persistent undertone," Mumford wrote in his autobiography, "I realized as never before how the insolence of his genius sometimes repelled me."[88] Still, when Mumford reviewed the exhibition in a lengthy, two-part series for the *New Yorker*, he was typically even-handed: generous in his praise of the architect's originality and critical of the architect's unwillingness to accommodate his clients' needs or to acknowledge his peers' influence. The initial piece examined Wright's residential work. Mumford opened with a paean to the architect:

> By almost universal acclaim, Frank Lloyd Wright is the most original architect the United States has produced, and—what is even more important—he is one of the most creative architectural geniuses of all time. Today, aged eighty-four, he is the Fujiyama of American architecture, at once a lofty mountain and a national shrine, a volcanic genius that may at any moment erupt with a new plan or a hitherto unimagined design for a familiar sort of building.[89]

But later in the piece, Mumford finally stated what had long remained unsaid about his professional—and by implication, his personal—relationship with the architect:

> This very quality of personality, so richly interfused in all of Wright's buildings, imposes a great burden upon criticism; one cannot possibly criticize his buildings without making an estimate of his personality, and reckoning with his idiosyncrasies as well as his gifts.[90]

Mumford was particularly critical of the architect's unwillingness to incorporate his clients' wishes into the design process, making a veiled stab at the Hanna House (1935) in Palo Alto, whose unrelenting hexagonal design he knew personally, having lived there briefly while teaching at Stanford University.

Wright, initially in favor of Mumford publishing an evaluation, was indignant over his first piece, and he was doubly indignant over his follow-up letter that closed with the phrase "as from one Master to another."[91] At a breakfast talk given to the fellowship, Wright elaborated:

> Well, he's master of the pen, yes. I'm not begrudging him that or denying it to him, but I am saying that the master of the pen has all down the centuries almost invariably and infallibly been wrong. That being master of the pen doesn't make you right.... And being a master of the pen doesn't save him, anymore than being a master of the straight line and the flat plane by way of the labor union and the concrete block, etc. makes me infallible. That's my liability. A man's mastership is at the same time his means, his opportunity and his menace.[92]

Wright was further angered by Mumford's second and final piece that appeared in the *New Yorker* two weeks later. This focused on Wright's public buildings, which, according to Mumford, occasionally suffered from the same fixation on geometric form as the architect's houses. Wright, Mumford noted dryly, "turns the polygon into a paragon."[93] Mumford further chided the architect for his anti-urban outlook, most cogently expressed in Broadacre City, and for his continued political and architectural isolationism from global, or universal, currents:

> While Wright is sound in asserting the American architect's freedom from colonial servility, it is another thing for him to denounce architects of European origin, such men of integrity and human understanding as Gropius, in language (and thought) that should be reserved for morbidly isolationist journals. The America First streak in Wright is a coarse, dark vein in the fine granite of his mind, and it had kept him from learning as much as he might have from those who by taste and temperament and training most differed from him.[94]

Yet, despite this harsh appraisal, Mumford recognized that Wright, more than any other living architect, best expressed the potential of modern architecture to develop along with the needs of post–World War II society:

> The fact remains that in a period of specialist constrictions and nationalist conformities his lifework has expressed the full gamut of *human* scale, from mathematics to poetry, from pure form to pure feeling, from the regional to the planetary, from the personal to the cosmic. In an age intimidated by

its successes and depressed by a series of disasters, he awakens, by his still confident example, a sense of the fullest *human* possibilities. What Wright has achieved as an individual in isolated buildings, conceived in "the nature of materials," our whole community, if it takes fire from his creativity, may eventually achieve in common designs growing more fully out of "the nature of man."[95]

Together, the two pieces wounded Wright deeply, perhaps because he had always considered Mumford to be a loyal admirer and friend rather than a critic of independent convictions. Wright composed an angry but heartfelt retort to Mumford in which he rehashed the old "communism versus democracy" argument, but ultimately decided against sending it. "Llewis!" he wrote at the end of the unsent letter. "What really hurts is to know that you—to whom I have looked with hope and love—should understand my work so much in reverse."[96]

Mumford did not learn of Wright's despair.[97] The correspondence continued amicably for another five years. Despite impassioned pleas, Lewis and Sophia Mumford never visited Taliesin, not even for the birthday celebrations leading up to Wright's ninth decade. The proclamation of October 17, 1956 as "Frank Lloyd Wright Day" in Chicago provided another opportunity for the two to meet, but Mumford refused the architect's invitation to preside over the evening banquet, believing that the event was intended solely to publicize Wright's "Mile-High Skyscraper" project. "In that project all of Wright's egocentric weaknesses were crystallized in an ultimate fantasy," Mumford wrote in his autobiography, "conceived as if by a lineal descendent of Kublai Khan."[98] King Lear might have been a more apt comparison, for Wright, nearing the end of a long and productive life, wished only to draw those whom he loved—and offended—near to him again. Significantly, their last exchange of letters focused on the design of the Wainwright Tomb in St. Louis, a work that Wright had sketched at their reconciliation luncheon, and that had long been attributed to Louis Sullivan. According to an unpublished manuscript that Wright asked Mumford to review, Wright credits himself with the overall design, attributing only the ornament to "*lieber Meister*":

[Hugh] Morrison came up with the Wainwright tomb as Sullivan's Masterpiece. A work I had myself laid out for L. H. S. to see on my own

> drawing-board. It was least Sullivan. But, the master liked it and I was thrilled to see him draw most of the ornamental details with his own hand.[99]

In the summer of 1958 Wright suffered a slight stroke, but by the beginning of autumn he had fully recovered, and it seemed that he was unstoppable. Thirty-one new commissions came in to his office that year, with over 150 on the boards at different stages. The outer formwork was removed from the concrete exterior of the Guggenheim Museum, revealing the great ramp rising on Manhattan's Fifth Avenue to an astonished public. Wright would not live to see it completed, however. He died on April 9, 1959, two months short of his ninety-second birthday.

Moved by the passing of his old friend, Mumford, who was then in residence at the University of Pennsylvania, delivered an extemporaneous lecture on Wright's life and work the very next day. In his autobiography, he wrote:

> I must admit that my Wright lecture came near to being... "total criticism," since I did not spare myself any more than I spared Wright.... And even if the words had been recorded on tape, the lecture itself, with its passion, its exuberance, its harassing search for truth, likewise in my self-exposure and self-criticism, which underlay the very words I addressed to Wright, would all be missing. This was not a psychoanalytic diagnosis: it was a dramatic act, set within the vast theater of Wright's own genius. If that was not to be my last word on Frank Lloyd Wright, it deserved to be.[100]

But this was not to be Mumford's last word. In December 1959, Mumford delivered a mixed review of Wright's completed Guggenheim Museum, admiring its dynamic enclosure of space, but faulting the peculiarities of its exhibition areas.[101] The following year, however, Mumford delivered a final, more generous appraisal in an obituary written for the American Academy of Arts and Letters, an esteemed organization to which both he and Wright belonged. "One of our giant redwoods has fallen," Mumford wrote at the beginning of the piece, "and left a space we cannot fill by any quick plantation of lesser trees."[102]

Mumford lived another thirty years. Wright's death created a void in Mumford's metaphorical forest that, in fact, could not be filled. No contemporary architect's work embodied as fully the organic and human principles Mumford advocated for a society increasingly seduced by modern technology. Moreover, Mumford had no close friends left in the architectural profession except for his aging colleagues in the Regional Planning Association of America.

Mumford's criticism had no discernable effect on Wright's architecture. Nevertheless, as a reading of their correspondence makes abundantly clear, Wright valued Mumford's friendship and approbation just as Mumford was inspired by Wright's life and work. Both men, moreover, had a strongly similar iconoclastic streak that galvanized as much as it irritated the architecture profession. If the two could not draw closer together in friendship, it was perhaps because they were fundamentally and temperamentally too much alike. Notwithstanding their political differences and their divergent views on cities and other matters, Wright and Mumford, once their friendship had been reestablished, consistently manifested a respect for each other, and more: a deep and abiding affection, as their letters testify. Their concern for each other also encompassed their families. Mumford recognized Olgivanna Wright's influence on her husband, as Wright recognized Sophia Mumford's strength. To both men—ideas, words, buildings, and above all—people mattered.

Wright never forgot the debt he owed Mumford when the critic wrote favorably about the architect's true worth—at a time when Wright was seemingly alone among his professional peers and under intense public scrutiny over his complicated personal life. By the time of his death, Wright had earned worldwide recognition. He had come to be regarded as the century's seminal architect, just as Mumford would later come to be regarded as the century's seminal architecture critic. Both Wright and Mumford embraced the ideal that architecture could revitalize an increasingly fragmented modern society. They fought vigorously in favor of an organic architecture adapted to human need and the natural and regional environment and against the seemingly monolithic, impersonal forms of the International Style. The exchange of words and ideas that follows considerably enriches—and humanizes—the discourse surrounding American architecture in the twentieth century.

NOTES

1 Frank Lloyd Wright, *An Autobiography* (London: Longmans, Green and Company, 1932) is the architect's own idiosyncratic account of his life. An expanded and revised edition was published by Duell, Sloan and Pearce, New York, in 1943. The scholarly bibliography on Wright is extensive. For the fullest combined account of his life and work, see Neil Levine, *The Architecture of Frank Lloyd Wright* (Princeton, New Jersey: Princeton University Press, 1996).

2 For an early discussion of the "organic," see Frank Lloyd Wright, "In the Cause of Architecture: Second Paper," *Architectural Record* 35 (May 1914): 405–413.

3 Frank Lloyd Wright, *Ausgeführte Bauten und Entwürfe von Frank Lloyd Wright* [Berlin: Ernst Wasmuth, 1910].

4 Lewis Mumford, *Sketches From Life: The Autobiography of Lewis Mumford, The Early Years* (New York: Dial Press, 1982) covers Mumford's life through World War II. Chapter 30 contains a lengthy account of Mumford's friendship with Wright. For a full biographical account of Mumford, see Donald L. Miller, *Lewis Mumford: A Life* (New York: Weidenfeld and Nicolson, 1989). On Mumford as critic of architecture and urbanism, see Robert Wojtowicz, *Lewis Mumford and American Modernism: Eutopian Theories for Architecture and Urban Planning* (Cambridge: Cambridge University Press, 1996).

5 See *Lewis Mumford and Patrick Geddes: The Correspondence*, edited and introduced by Frank G. Novak, Jr. (London: Routledge, 1995).

6 Ebenezer Howard, *Garden Cities of To-morrow* (London: Swan, Sonnenschein and Company, 1902).

7 Lewis Mumford, review of *Architecture and Democracy*, by Claude Bragdon, *Dial* 67 (4 October 1919): 318.

8 Lewis Mumford, *The Story of Utopias* (New York: Boni and Liveright, 1922).

9 On the Regional Planning Association of America, see Edward K. Spann, *Designing Modern America: The Regional Planning Association of America and Its Members* (Columbus: Ohio State University Press, 1996).

10 On Mumford's investigation into America's "usable past," see Alan Trachtenberg, "Mumford in the Twenties: The Historian as Artist," *Salmagundi* 49 (Summer 1980): 29–42.

11 Lewis Mumford, *Sticks and Stones: A Study of American Architecture and Civilization* (New York: Boni and Liveright, 1924).

12 Lewis Mumford, *Vom Blockhaus zum Wolkenkratzer: Eine Studie über Amerikanische Architektur und Zivilisation*, translated by M. Mauthner (Berlin: Bruno Cassirer Verlag, 1925).

13 Lewis Mumford, *The Golden Day: A Study in American Experience and Culture* (New York: Boni and Liveright, 1926).

14 Lewis Mumford, *Herman Melville* (New York: Harcourt, Brace and Company, 1929).

15 Lewis Mumford, *The Brown Decades: A Study of the Arts in America, 1865–1895* (New York: Harcourt, Brace and Company, 1931).

16 Mumford, *Sticks and Stones*, 181–182.

17 Lewis Mumford, "The Social Back Ground [*sic*] of Frank Lloyd Wright," *Wendingen* 7 (1925): 65–79.
18 Mumford, *Sketches*, 432.
19 Mumford, "The Social Back Ground [*sic*] of Frank Lloyd Wright," 78.
20 Lewis Mumford, "The Poison of Good Taste," *American Mercury* 6 (September 1925): 92–94.
21 Photocopy of letter from Frank Lloyd Wright to Lewis Mumford, 7 August 1926, Lewis Mumford Papers (hereafter lmp), Annenberg Rare Book and Manuscript Library, University of Pennsylvania, Philadelphia, Pennsylvania.
22 Letter from Lewis Mumford to Frank Lloyd Wright, 23 August 1926, The Frank Lloyd Wright Archives (hereafter flwa), The Frank Lloyd Wright Foundation, Taliesin West, Scottsdale, Arizona.
23 Mumford, *Sketches*, 432–433.
24 Lewis Mumford, "New York *vs.* Chicago in Architecture," *Architecture* 56 (November 1927): 241.
25 Ibid.
26 Mumford, *Sketches*, 433.
27 Frank Lloyd Wright, *Modern Architecture, Being the Kahn Lectures for 1930* (Princeton, New Jersey: Princeton University Press, 1931).
28 Wright, *An Autobiography*.
29 Lewis Mumford, "What Has 1932 Done for Literature?" *Atlantic Monthly* 150 (December 1932): 762.
30 Frank Lloyd Wright, *The Disappearing City* (New York: William Farquhar Payson, 1932).
31 Photocopy of letter from Frank Lloyd Wright to Lewis Mumford, 30 April 1928, lmp.
32 Letter from Lewis Mumford to Frank Lloyd Wright, 1 July 1930, flwa; letter from Lewis Mumford to Frank Lloyd Wright, 29 March 1931, flwa.
33 Photocopy of letter from Frank Lloyd Wright to Lewis Mumford, 7 July 1930, lmp; photocopy of letter from Frank Lloyd Wright to Lewis Mumford, 7 April 1931, lmp.
34 Lewis Mumford, "The Brown Decades: Architecture," *Scribner's* 89 (April 1931): 385–395.
35 Mumford, *Brown Decades*, 168–169.
36 Ibid., 173.
37 Photocopy of letter from Frank Lloyd Wright to Lewis Mumford, 9 December 1931, lmp.
38 Photocopy of letter from Frank Lloyd Wright to Lewis Mumford, 7 July 1930, lmp.
39 Lewis Mumford, "Two Chicago Fairs," *New Republic* 65 (21 January 1931): 272.
40 Frank Lloyd Wright, *An Autobiography*, revised edition (New York: Duell, Sloan and Pearce, 1943): 352.
41 On the history of the *Modern Architecture: International Exhibition*, see Terence Riley, *The International Style: Exhibition 15 and the Museum of Modern Art* (New York: Rizzoli, 1992).

42 Letter from Lewis Mumford to Frank Lloyd Wright, 29 March 1931, flwa.
43 Letter from Philip Johnson to Frank Lloyd Wright, 1 April 1931, flwa.
44 Photocopy of letter from Frank Lloyd Wright to Lewis Mumford, 19 January 1932, lmp.
45 Telegram from Lewis Mumford to Frank Lloyd Wright, 21 January 1932, flwa.
46 Photocopy of telegram from Frank Lloyd Wright to Lewis Mumford, 21 January 1932, lmp.
47 Letter from Lewis Mumford to Frank Lloyd Wright, 6 February 1932, flwa; Lewis Mumford, "Housing," in *Modern Architecture: International Exhibition* (New York: Museum of Modern Art, 1932): 179–191.
48 On Mumford's involvement with the *New Yorker*, see Robert Wojtowicz, "Introduction," in *Sidewalk Critic: Lewis Mumford's Writings on New York*, edited by Robert Wojtowicz (New York: Princeton Architectural Press, 1998): 11–29.
49 Lewis Mumford, "The Sky Line: Organic Architecture," *New Yorker* 8 (27 February 1932): 45.
50 Letter from Lewis Mumford to Frank Lloyd Wright, c. June 1932, flwa.
51 Photocopy of letter from Frank Lloyd Wright to Lewis Mumford, 9 December 1931, lmp.
52 Photocopy of letter from Frank Lloyd Wright to Lewis Mumford, 1 February 1932, lmp.
53 Letter from Lewis Mumford to Frank Lloyd Wright, 6 February 1932, flwa.
54 Lewis Mumford, "The Sky Line: Mr. Wright's City—Downtown Dignity," *New Yorker* 11 (27 April 1935): 64.
55 Ibid.
56 Photocopy of letter from Frank Lloyd Wright to Lewis Mumford, 27 April 1935, lmp; letter from Lewis Mumford to Frank Lloyd Wright, 25 June 1935, flwa.
57 Lewis Mumford, "The Sky Line: At Home, Indoors and Out," *New Yorker* 13 (12 February 1938): 31.
58 "Usonian Architect," *Time* 31 (17 January 1938): 29–32.
59 Frank Lloyd Wright, *An Organic Architecture: The Architecture of Democracy* (London: Lund Humphries, 1939).
60 *Two Great Americans: Frank Lloyd Wright, American Architect, and D. W. Griffith, American Film Master*, exhibition, Museum of Modern Art, New York, 13 November 1940 to 5 January 1941; Henry-Russell Hitchcock, Jr., *In the Nature of Materials: 1887–1941, The Buildings of Frank Lloyd Wright* (New York: Duell, Sloan and Pearce, 1942).
61 *Frank Lloyd Wright on Architecture: Selected Writings, 1894–1940*, edited with an introduction by Frederick Gutheim (New York: Duell, Sloan and Pearce, 1941).
62 Lewis Mumford, *Technics and Civilization* (New York: Harcourt, Brace and Company, 1934); Lewis Mumford, *The Culture of Cities* (New York: Harcourt, Brace and Company, 1938).
63 Mumford, *Technics*, 370.
64 Photocopy of letter from Frank Lloyd Wright to Lewis Mumford, 6 August 1934, lmp.

65 Mumford, *Culture*, caption to plate 30.
66 "Form of Forms," *Time* 31 (18 April 1938): 40–43.
67 Lewis Mumford, *The South in Architecture* (New York: Harcourt, Brace and Company, 1941).
68 Letter from Lewis Mumford to Frank Lloyd Wright, 2 April 1941, flwa.
69 Lewis Mumford, *Men Must Act* (New York: Harcourt, Brace and Company, 1939); Lewis Mumford, *Faith for Living* (New York: Harcourt, Brace and Company, 1940).
70 Letter from Frank Lloyd Wright to Matt Walton, 1 March 1945, flwa.
71 Frank Lloyd Wright, "Of What Use Is a Great Navy with No Place to Hide?" *A Taliesin Square-Paper*, 2 (May 1941), reprinted in *Frank Lloyd Wright: Collected Writings, Volume 4, 1939–1949*, edited by Bruce Pfeiffer with an introduction by Kenneth Frampton (New York: Rizzoli in association with the Frank Lloyd Wright Foundation, 1994): 74.
72 Letter from Lewis Mumford to Frank Lloyd Wright, 30 May 1941, flwa.
73 Photocopy of letter from Frank Lloyd Wright to Lewis Mumford, 3 Jun 1941, lmp.
74 Mumford, *Sketches*, 436.
75 Lewis Mumford, "Frank Lloyd Wright's Defeatism Aids Slave Empire—Mumford," *New Leader* 24 (14 June 1941): 8.
76 Frank Lloyd Wright, "Mumford Lectures," review of *The South in Architecture* by Lewis Mumford, *Saturday Review of Architecture* 24 (23 August 1941): 16.
77 Letter from Lewis Mumford to John Gould Fletcher, 10 April 1946, Special Collections Department, University of Arkansas Libraries, Fayetteville, Arkansas.
78 Frank Lloyd Wright, *The Sovereignty of the Individual: In the Cause of Architecture*, privately printed, 1951; reprint of preface to Frank Lloyd Wright, *Ausgeführte Bauten und Entwürfe von Frank Lloyd Wright*.
79 Lewis Mumford, *The Condition of Man* (New York: Harcourt, Brace and Company, 1944); Lewis Mumford, *The Conduct of Life* (New York: Harcourt, Brace and Company, 1951).
80 Lewis Mumford, *Green Memories: The Story of Geddes Mumford* (New York: Harcourt, Brace and Company, 1947).
81 Lewis Mumford, *Sticks and Stones: A Study of American Architecture and Civilization*, revised edition (New York: Dover Publications, 1955); Lewis Mumford, *The Brown Decades: A Study of the Arts in America, 1865–1895*, revised edition (New York: Dover Publications, 1955); *Roots of Contemporary Architecture: A Series of Thirty-Seven Essays from the Mid-Nineteenth Century to the Present*, edited with an introduction by Lewis Mumford (New York: Reinhold Publishing Co., 1952); Lewis Mumford, *The Transformations of Man* (New York: Harper & Bros., 1956); Lewis Mumford, *The City in History: Its Origins, Its Transformations, and Its Prospects* (New York: Harcourt, Brace and Company, 1961).
82 Mumford, *Sketches*, 436. Here Mumford is referring to his book *The Conduct of Life*; in the text of *Sketches*, he mistakenly attributes the print to Hokusai, another well-known Japanese artist.

83 Lewis Mumford, *Art and Technics* (New York: Columbia University Press, 1952).
84 Letter from Lewis Mumford to Frank Lloyd Wright, 2 February 1952, flwa.
85 Photocopy of letter from Frank Lloyd Wright to Lewis Mumford, 10 January 1952, lmp.
86 Frank Lloyd Wright, "The Art and Craft of the Machine," in *Roots*, 169–185.
87 *The Future of Architecture* (New York: Horizon Press, 1953); *The Natural House* (New York: Horizon Press, 1954); *An American Architecture*, edited by Edgar Kaufmann, Jr. (New York: Horizon Press, 1955); *The Story of the Tower: The Tree that Escaped the Forest* (New York: Horizon Press, 1956); *A Testament* (New York: Horizon Press, 1957); *The Living City* (New York: Horizon Press, 1958); *Drawings for a Living Architecture* (New York: Horizon Press with the Bear Run Foundation Inc. and the Edgar J. Kaufmann Charitable Foundation, 1959).
88 Mumford, *Sketches*, 437.
89 Lewis Mumford, "The Sky Line: A Phoenix Too Infrequent," *New Yorker* 29 (28 November 1953): 133.
90 Ibid.
91 Letter from Lewis Mumford to Frank Lloyd Wright, 3 December 1953, lmp.
92 Frank Lloyd Wright, transcription of audiotaped breakfast talk to the Taliesin Fellowship, 6 December 1953, flwa, reel 84A.
93 Lewis Mumford, "The Sky Line: A Phoenix Too Infrequent—II," *New Yorker* 29 (12 December 1953): 119.
94 Ibid., 125.
95 Ibid., 127.
96 Unsent letter from Frank Lloyd Wright to Lewis Mumford, 18 December 1953, flwa.
97 Mumford wrote in his autobiography, "[Wright] made no comment on my second article, despite its unsparing severity." Mumford, *Sketches*, 438.
98 Mumford, *Sketches*, 439.
99 Frank Lloyd Wright, unpublished revision to Sixth Book of *An Autobiography*, flwa, AV#2401.384. Hugh Morrison was Sullivan's biographer.
100 Mumford, *Sketches*, 440.
101 Lewis Mumford, "The Sky Line: What Wright Hath Wrought," *New Yorker* 35 (5 December 1959): 105–129.
102 Lewis Mumford, "Frank Lloyd Wright, 1869–1959," in American Academy of Arts and Letters and the National Institute of Arts and Letters, *Proceedings*, 2d series, no. 10 (1960), 382.

24 MAY 1982

RE: FRANK LLOYD WRIGHT

Before letting . . . [the dealer] take away our copy of the *Wendingen* issue on Wright and the French (in French) Catalogue of a Wright exhibition, I copied out Lewis's evaluation of Wright, which was written all over the front cover of the catalogue.

Wright had been indignant against Henry-Russell Hitchcock's introduction to the show, and had scribbled his comments all over the pages, in pencil, appealing to Lewis for sympathy. This was dated 6 November 1928.

S. M. [Sophia Mumford]

6 NOVEMBER 1928 NOTES BY L. M.

"Wright's art is prophetic. It does not simply conform and adjust. It reacts and makes new demands. It lies in the future: it cannot be the dominant art today because our times are not favorable to such an art. We demand the unhesitating conformity of the engineer, who had independent values of his own."

"Those whom Hitchcock calls the New Pioneers have restored the classical formulae: they have reinvented the five orders, now orders of engineering, and whoever steps out of their narrow frame commits heresy and commits a breach of taste. The coldness and dryness of 18th[-]Century architecture is, here again, with a touch of hardness further added by our own mechanical methods. The form is often excellent: what is lacking is the element of feeling, of the gesture made for the sake of a certain human reaction, feeling, and place-sense, the sense of fitness, of harmonious interaction with the environment."

"Wright has these qualities in abundance for he has tact—the tact of an artist with materials and a love of nature, with the earth—of a man who wants all men to live humanely. Hence the garden which surrounds and completes all that Wright does."

A NOTE ABOUT THE CORRESPONDENCE

The letters written by Lewis Mumford to Frank Lloyd Wright are part of the Frank Lloyd Wright Foundation Archives at Taliesin West in Scottsdale, Arizona. Some typed copies of these letters may be found in the Lewis Mumford Papers, which are deposited in the Annenberg Rare Book and Manuscript Library at the University of Pennsylvania in Philadelphia, Pennsylvania.

The letters written by Frank Lloyd Wright to Lewis Mumford, along with some ephemeral Wright materials, were sold by Lewis and Sophia Mumford to a manuscript dealer around 1983. Fortunately, the Mumfords had made photocopies of the letters and most of the inscriptions on the ephemeral materials before they were dispersed; these photocopies are located in the Annenberg Rare Book and Manuscript Library. For unknown reasons, one original letter by Wright to Mumford was not sold; it is deposited in the Annenberg Rare Book and Manuscript Library. Two original letters by Wright to Mumford have since surfaced at the James S. Copley Library in La Jolla, California. Furthermore, Wright made carbon copies of many letters to Mumford, which are located in the Wright Foundation Archives. Unless otherwise noted, the editors have assumed that Mumford received all letters from Wright, even when they only exist in carbon-copy form.

The letter from Lewis Mumford to John Gould Fletcher is part of the holdings of the Special Collections Department of the University of Arkansas Libraries, Fayetteville.

Except for minor corrections, the correspondents' original punctuation has been transcribed exactly as written.

Key to abbreviations:

ms = manuscript
ts = typescript
pc = photocopy
cc = carbon copy
flwa = Frank Lloyd Wright Archives
lmp = Lewis Mumford Papers
jscl = James S. Copley Library
uarlf = University of Arkansas Libraries, Fayetteville

1926–1929

Frank Lloyd Wright and Lewis Mumford begin corresponding during the greatest building boom the United States had yet experienced. Wright, with his individualistic, organic approach to architecture, belongs to none of the current camps of architects and, furthermore, the few buildings he designs during this decade are located far from the real-estate epicenter of New York City. Subsequently, his work is largely ignored by his peers and by architectural critics. Mumford is the exception. A young, New York-based journalist, Mumford created a sensation with his 1924 book, *Sticks and Stones*, in which he undertook a social analysis of American architecture and found most of it wanting. Although he has not yet seen Wright's work in person, he recognizes in it an original streak that contributes significantly to modern life and that stands apart from the prevailing "poison of good taste."

The initial exchange of letters between Wright and Mumford occurs in August 1926 and the two first meet in person in January 1927. Not until 1928, however, does the correspondence gain momentum. Although Wright is nearly thirty years Mumford's senior, the two men establish common ground quickly on a variety of matters, ranging from the professional to the personal. The letters also touch on such major figures in American architecture as Fiske Kimball, Henry-Russell

Hitchcock, Jr., and Douglas Haskell, and on the group of European modern architects who are beginning to gain attention stateside, including Le Corbusier and Walter Gropius. Wright floats the idea of a school to be built around his organic design principles. He also invites Mumford and his family to Taliesin, his compound in southern Wisconsin, but Mumford declines.

Dear Lewis Mumford,

I want to tell you how much I liked your "Poison of Good Taste" in the *Mercury*.[1]

It was so clear and sound.

Your pen seems pointed in the right direction and could I wield mine as effectively I might be a better champion of a cause where I am confined to a hod of mortar and some bricks—as the matter stands.

I have been interested in reading my "obituaries" in *WENDINGEN*.[2] The heart and brain of my work is apparently effectually concealed by thought—The language in which I architecturally clothe mine seems to have been a successful disguise—which none of my critics have penetrated.

Your article was interesting and sensible until you touched me and then you seemed to be trying to do the fair thing by something you did not quite understand and reluctantly sympathized with "on principle"—[3]

I think if we were to "walk and talk" together a little your judgement might be in a similar direction but different. It struck me as somewhat "diffident."

A "poet in architecture" means something not included in the estimates of my generously inclined colleagues—when they turn critic—, if I am to be trusted. But I am grateful just the same.

You can be of great service to <u>an ideal</u>, the one that has persisted since time began and must prevail, for it is Nature raised to the nth power. This "ideal" that is now, as before, and will be, swamped by a little brief authority. <u>The ideal</u> will take care of itself—it always has done so—. But if only someone could take care of the fools who waste our birthright as a "free people" in this rash mortgage they forge, to be paid by posterity with usurous interest. They "blow in" the proceeds therefore on the masquerade with us more than a half-hearted false-pride gratified, to show for it.

---

1 Lewis Mumford, "The Poison of Good Taste," *American Mercury* 6 (September 1925): 92–94.

2 *Wendingen* 7; bound together as *The Life-Work of the American Architect Frank Lloyd Wright*, edited by H. Th. Wijdeveld (Santpoort, Holland: C. A. Mees, 1925).

3 Lewis Mumford, "The Social Back Ground [*sic*] of Frank Lloyd Wright," *Wendingen* 7 (1925): 65–79.

We are agreed on many matters in principle, I am not one of them but am

Faithfully yours,
[signed]
Frank Lloyd Wright
Taliesin[4] Aug. 7th, 26

[pc ms lmp]

4 Frank Lloyd Wright, Taliesin (architect's residence and studio), Spring Green, Wisconsin, begun 1911. Taliesin is Welsh for "shining brow."

THE MAPLES
AMENIA, NEW YORK

23 AUGUST 1926

Dear Frank Lloyd Wright:

Your letter was very welcome; for I have been on the point of writing you more than once; and this gives me my opportunity.

Your comments on my *Wendingen* essay are quite accurate. I had doubts as to whether I ought to write the essay at all, not because I am lukewarm in admiration; but because, unfortunately, I have not yet been west, and have not yet seen your work. Photographs are useful only as shorthand memoranda: the building itself is usually much better or much worse than the photograph. What you felt in my article was, assuredly, timidity; but this was occasioned not by a failure to grasp your work but by an ingrained distrust of saying anything about buildings I had not seen and walked around and gotten into.

Professor Lorch has asked me to lecture at the University of Michigan this coming winter: and one of my reasons for accepting this engagement is my desire to see the actual examples of your work.[1] I trust this will also enable us to meet. It was brash of me to write about your work at all for *Wendingen*; but when I get out a new edition of *Sticks and Stones*, after I've become genuinely acquainted with it, you may trust me to make amends.[2]

It seems to me, at a distance, that most of the foreign critics have misinterpreted you by reading into your work a rigorous mechanistic tendency which, in fact, you have passed beyond. They have merely caught up with the machine; whereas you have carried the machine, as it were, into a new phase. Is this misreading you, too? Ernst May's enthusiasm for your work when he returned from Chicago greatly reassured me; for he is a humane fellow, and has no obsessions, and knows what men and women and children need to be happy![3]

---

1 Emil Lorch (1870–1963), painter, architect, and educator, who was instrumental in creating and shaping the College of Architecture at the University of Michigan.

2 Lewis Mumford, *Sticks and Stones: A Study of American Architecture and Civilization* (New York: Boni and Liveright, 1924).

3 Ernst May (1886–1970), German architect and planner.

I am grateful for the impulse that prompted your letter.

Faithfully yours,
[signed]
Lewis Mumford

[ts flwa]

[TELEGRAM]

Received at 267 EIGHTH AVE
N143 51 BLUE.SPRINGGREEN, WIS 21 1149A
1927 OCT 21 PM 2 59

ROBERT M LOVETT, CARE: *NEW REPUBLIC.*[1]
21 ST.

CIRCUMSTANCES LEAVE ME ALONE AND LONESOME FOR SEVERAL WEEKS[.] COME UP WITH LEWIS MUMFORD AND BRING YOUR WIVES AND CHILDREN FOR A WEEK OR TWO AND DO YOUR WORK HERE[.] BEAUTY OF COUNTRYSIDE AND HOME INTOXICATING[.] EXPENSE OF TRIP NO MORE THAN A FEW EVENING[S] IN NEW YORK[.] FORGET THE *NEW REPUBLIC.*[2]

[pc lmp]

---

1 Robert Morss Lovett (1870–1956), American editor.
2 Invitation declined by Lovett. See letter from Robert Morss Lovett to Frank Lloyd Wright, 26 October 1927, Frank Lloyd Wright Archives (hereafter flwa), Taliesin West, Scottsdale, Arizona.

ALBERT CHASE MCARTHUR[1]
ARCHITECT
311 WEST JEFFERSON STREET
PHOENIX
ARIZONA

APRIL 30TH, 1928

Mr. Lewis Mumford,
4112 Gosman Avenue,
Long Island City, N.Y.

My dear Lewis Mumford:—

Fiske Kimball has just sent me a copy of his new book,—a well written brief for the "Classic" bracketing McKim, Meade [*sic*] and White's thought in Architecture with Lewis [*sic*] Sullivan's.[2] God save the mark! And this is "History."

It would be hard to beat that for grave-robbing, I say. I write this because of a note from the Century Company, asking for views of "Taliesin" to illustrate your article on "American Architecture" in which you make "a kindly reference to me."[3] (See copy of enclosed letter to Fiske Kimball).

I am heartily sick of the historical falsifying of the real course of ideas in the Architecture of our Country, unconsciously done as most of it is. A true concept of "modernism" in origin or effect is so far almost wholly lacking. Why don't you record it? No man has yet stood up to the task, learning anything further West of Manhattan,—the commercialized monstrosity,—than Buffalo, New York.

Why not you? Come afield and see for yourself the healthy undergrowth coming through this rank obscuring growth of pseudo-classic weeds. A healthy undergrowth rising from seed planted in the prairie

---

1 Albert Chase McArthur (1881–1951), American architect. [Wright is associated with McArthur at this time as a consultant on the Arizona Biltmore Resort project and is using his letterhead.]

2 Fiske Kimball (1888–1955), American architect, historian, and museum director; McKim, Mead & White, American architectural firm based in New York; Louis H. Sullivan (1856–1924), American architect and onetime employer of Frank Lloyd Wright.

3 Lewis Mumford, "American Architecture To-day: II," *Architecture* 57 (June 1928): 301–308.

soil thirty years ago? Pseudo classic has only been a "cover crop" as the farmers say, for that future harvesting!

You will write what you please, as you please, but until you have "come" afield, "led by myself," you will not write with more than the artist's instinct which is dangerous in a historian, unless based upon the fundamental acts contributing to the subject he views and records. Pardon the seeming attempt to "preach." It is perhaps uncalled for and an egotistic assumption on my part, but I am just smarting from Fiske Kimball's well-meant "obituary." Why allow Corbusier—et al to "beard us" in our own den?[4]

Faithfully yours,
[signed]
Frank Lloyd Wright

[pc ts&ms lmp]

---

4 Le Corbusier, a.k.a. Charles-Edouard Jeanneret (1887–1965), Swiss architect and planner.

[SENT TO LEWIS MUMFORD][1]

APRIL 30TH, 1928

Mr. Fiske Kimball,
Pennsylvania Museum of Fine Art
Philadelphia, Pennsylvania

Dear Fiske Kimball:—

A copy of your attractive new book came to hand, forwarded to me here in the Desert yesterday.[2]

I have been reading my obituaries to a considerable extent the past year or two, and think, with Mark Twain, the reports of my death greatly exaggerated.

You were very kind to me though you used me to point your moral and adorn your tale, and left me in exile. Yours was no donkey's kick at a "dying lion." Nor am I a lion, nor dying, nor am I in exile.

Sometime let someone come far enough away from Manhattan to mark what the thought-built houses they called the "New School of the Middle West" have done (consciously or unconsciously) to three out of five buildings from Buffalo to Los Angeles, quietening the sky-line, broadening and strengthening the mass, ordering the openings, reducing the "fancy features," marrying all of them to the ground to some extent, and be convinced of the potency in America of those ideas. Those ideas are more potent today than ever before, though their origin is growing obscure in the flood of pseudo-classic. This to offset inevitable abuse.

A lost cause? "The Triumph of the Classic"? Dear man! The cornice has gone. The Larkin Building, about which you write so well, struck it fast.[3] No cornice, no classic! Life goes on! From your honorable niche in the museum in conservative Old Philadelphia, does that ancient dream "The Classic" still possess and obsess you? Or are you

1 Published in "American Architecture: Correspondence of Walter Pach, Paul Cret, Frank Lloyd Wright and Erich Mendelsohn with Fiske Kimball," *Architectural Record* 65 (May 1929): 431–434.

2 Fiske Kimball, *American Architecture* (Indianapolis and New York: Bobbs-Merrill, 1928).

3 Frank Lloyd Wright, Larkin Company Administration Building, Buffalo, New York, 1903.

merely comforting the abstraction that was lost at the Columbian exposition thirty-two years ago,—lost—because it was only again reborn to be commercialized.[4] Trying to make it open its lips, eyes it never had,—and seem to speak?

You write well, so well. I think we need you in the constructive movement. I intend to take the pains to enlist your pen in behalf of the nature of the thing—as architecture—whereas the nature of the thing as practiced is what you have been talking about—and how!

Meantime my best to you, faithfully. You are a friendly enemy. They make ultimately the best friends.

[pc cc ts lmp]

---

4 World's Columbian Exposition (World's Fair), Chicago, 1893.

4002 LOCUST STREET
LONG ISLAND CITY, N.Y.

11 MAY 1928

Dear Frank Lloyd Wright:

Your letters and your photos came very happily: the latter just in time for inclusion in my second article for *Architecture*. The reference to your work there is inadequate, partly because I spent so much energy in damning everybody else's; but I promised Lee Simonson to do a full dress article on your work next fall, for *Creative Art*; and if you will let me keep the photos till then I shall be very grateful.[1] I saw your work in situ for the first time in 1927, as you perhaps know: my timidity in writing about it up to that time was based partly upon the fact that I hadn't seen it from four sides, and partly because I was woefully incapable of writing about anything except general tendencies. In my *Creative Art*'s article I shall try to get down to brass tacks. I sympathize with your feelings about Kimball: to me he is a very capable jackass, who is capable of grubbing together all sorts of good reasons for defending very bad things, and all sorts of bad reasons for attacking very good ones. Unfortunately, he is capable; and so can do a lot of damage. Your recent work has made my heart leap with joy: if it is work of a "dead one" the sooner the rest of us stop living the better. Your California houses should put the quietus upon those who want to wrap you in the mummy-cloth of a formula; they should, but nothing will stop people who prefer mummies to living bodies. As for most of your European admirers—good people though so many of them are—they fall into raptures over the articulated skeleton, and despise the flesh, whilst your work, being more whole than theirs, has skeleton, flesh, and all necessary organs, and so will be, I hope, the mold of all our new architecture. The young men are coming along well, though: you have plenty of admirers and followers and, best of all, understanders among them. So take heart. I wish I could take another trip through the West: but a hundred things prevent me—some of them equally attractive things, like the book I'm writing, some of them less attractive, the usual limitations of time and

1 Lee Simonson (1888–1967), American writer, editor, and painter.

money.[2] Before another year or so is out I hope to make the trip, however, clear to the coast. Good luck in the meanwhile!

Ever yours,
[signed]
Lewis Mumford

[ts flwa]

2 Lewis Mumford, *Herman Melville* (New York: Harcourt, Brace and Company, 1929).

[C. JUNE–JULY 1928]

Dear L. M.

This from the strongest paper on the "Coast" is better—[1]

It is a surprise too. I don't know who Millier is except that he edits the section of Art and Artists.[2] The "break" you see is coming all down the line!

To you!
[signed]
F.LLW

[pc ms lmp]

---

1 Unidentified article from *The Los Angeles Times*.

2 Arthur Millier (1893–1975), writer, editor, and painter.

AMENIA, NEW YORK

10 JULY 1928

Dear Frank Lloyd Wright:

Many hearty thanks for your letters, notes, & photographs: your comments have tamed Hitchcock's essay into a precious document: and I am happy to be the custodian of it![1] I have met Hitchcock & know that he heartily admires you: as for the conspiracy, it is wholly an unconscious one, although none the less depressing for that reason.[2] Hitchcock is a young man: an instructor in art at Vassar. He belongs to the post-war generation, and that, I think, is one of his main difficulties. Like the Frenchmen he admires, & like some of the Germans of the same guild, his esthetic ideas are biased by an inadequate sociology: he fancies that the age of art is over, and (like Spengler) he thinks the architecture of the future will be engineering or nothing.[3] This view is an expression of impotence, on the part of men who, like Gropius, are artists to their fingertips: they feel no "must" insides of them: so, unlike the academic impotents, they acknowledge their emptiness honestly.[4] Your work is necessarily a challenge to these men, as health & vigor is a challenge to the invalid: they excuse their own inability to go on with it, to develop it in response to their own situation, by affecting to regard your work as a fore-runner to their own. As I see it, things stand just the other way about. Root's & Sullivan's early skyscrapers are the equivalent of Corbusier's designs today: they are both primitives of the machine: while your work is a step beyond this, with fuller mastery of the materials & freer expression.[5] Expressed in time, you are still 30 years ahead of Corbusier. I shall say some of these things in the fall: but I am still trying to decide what form the article should take & where it should be published. The clipping you just sent

---

1 Most likely Mumford is referring to Henry-Russell Hitchcock, Jr., "The Decline of Architecture," *The Hound and the Horn* 1 (September): 28–35.

2 Henry-Russell Hitchcock, Jr. (1903–1986), American architectural historian, writer, and critic.

3 Oswald Spengler (1880–1936), German philosopher.

4 Walter Gropius (1883–1969), German architect and director of the Bauhaus (1919–1928). He subsequently headed the architecture school at Harvard from 1938 to 1952.

5 John Wellborn Root (1850–1891), American architect.

is very good criticism indeed. I am glad to know that such people are working on the coast. I am dickering with the Denver Art Museum over a course of six lectures they've almost invited me to give: so there's a chance that I may see more of your work—and more mid-American work generally.

Ever yours,
[signed]
Lewis Mumford

[ms flwa]

[PRINTED INVITATION]

MARRIED
AUGUST 25
RANCHO SANTA FE CALIFORNIA
OLGA IVANOVNA
DAUGHTER OF
IVAN LAZOVICH AND
MILITZA MILAN OF
CETTINJE MONTENEGRO
TO FRANK LLOYD WRIGHT
SON OF ANNA LLOYD-JONES
AND WILLIAM CARY WRIGHT
TALIESIN WISCONSIN 1928[1]

[pc lmp]

1 Olgivanna Lloyd Wright, née Lazovich (1896–1985), educator, author, philosopher, and third wife of Frank Lloyd Wright.

AMENIA, NEW YORK

24 SEPTEMBER 1928

Dear Frank Lloyd Wright,

Your telegram came to me while I was working on the hardest part of the biography I'm writing; and in the meanwhile a fortnight has gone by.[1] Forgive my delay in putting matters straight: but I have had a long and exhausting pull. This is how it all came about. In May I discussed with Lee Simonson a series of possible articles on architecture; among them was one that I proposed to do about you, and he put that at the head of the list. Douglas Haskell is a very able young writer, who became interested in architecture four or five years ago when he traveled abroad, and came back and edited a whacking, satirical number of the *New Student* on architecture in our colleges—for which I gave him various leads and suggestions.[2] During the last year, he has taken seriously to architectural criticism; and, since he is serious and very promising, I suggested to him that he go around to Simonson and have a talk with him, saying that I was quite willing to relinquish any of my subjects if he felt that he could handle them. He is a genuine admirer of yours; and arranged to do the article on you—for Simonson wanted to lead off with that this autumn, and I had told him that I would be out of commission for a while. I was not aware that this arrangement had been made definite till Haskell wrote me in the middle of the summer to ask me for more photographs. I accepted it gladly, however, first because *Creative Art* could not give me enough space to write a thorough article about your work and ideas, second, because I was busy with my Melville and could not return to architecture till this fall; and third, because I wanted Haskell to have a tip-top subject to sail into. I have not seen his article: but I am sure it will be an understanding one. It doesn't interfere with my own plans for writing about you in the slightest. There are three or four magazines that are pretty well open to anything I write; and when I get back to New York I shall put my ideas together for an article which might also serve as an introduction for an American book of your work, supposing it were wise to get

1 Telegram unlocated; Mumford, *Herman Melville*.

2 Douglas Haskell (1899–1979), American architectural critic.

such a book out. I can't promise any definite date for this yet: I am not through with Melville: and I need time to recuperate from that before undertaking anything that requires more than half-witted application; but I jolly well want to do it. Haskell is worth while encouraging: please bear with him. Bear with me, too, please: a book is the worst sort of pregnancy. Your wedding announcement was a very happy, as well as a very beautiful one; and I wish you all joy and serenity—and many great buildings!

Faithfully,
[signed]
Lewis Mumford

[ts&ms flwa]

Mr. Lewis Mumford
Amenia, New York

Dear Lewis Mumford:

You will be glad to know I am no longer walking the New York streets, hat in hand. Taliesin is regained.[1] We are established here, again at work,—interesting work,—not to brag about it, but to reassure you;—Working on the Desert-Resort Hotel in the simon-pure Arizona desert,[2]—half million dollar commission for Dr. Chandler at Chandler, Arizona near Phoenix,[3]—(cactus among the cacti), nearby where I established the textile-block construction in the "million dollar" Arizona Biltmore, now nearing completion;[4]—A new house in spirit and letter for my editor cousin at Tulsa, Oklahoma;[5]—A twenty-three story copper and glass apartment-tower for your barbaric New York City;—St. Mark's Tower in-the-Bouwerie;[6]—"the architect triumphant over the Machine,"—let us hope; a school-house for the Rosenwald Foundation,—you know,—the negroes in the South.[7] I have tried to make this one theirs. The Yankee things they have been getting seem to me rather hard on them: this is another modest excursion into the nature and feeling of an alien race such as was the Tokio [*sic*] hotel on a grand scale.[8]

Have also signed a life contract with Leerdam Glassfabriek to make glass designs for all sorts of things on a royalty basis.[9] Trying my hands at the arts and crafts, you see.

Read the prospectus of the school herewith and write me a "brief."[10] The University is already interested.[11] Your supporting word would

---

1 A reference to Wright's regaining control of Taliesin from his creditors.

2 San Marcos-in-the-Desert, near Phoenix, 1928.

3 Alexander Chandler (1859–1950), American developer.

4 Albert Chase McArthur with Frank Lloyd Wright (consultant), Arizona Biltmore Hotel, Phoenix, 1927.

5 Richard Lloyd Jones House, Tulsa, 1929.

6 St. Mark's-in-the-Bouwerie Project, New York City, 1929.

7 Rosenwald School Project, Hampton, Virginia, 1928.

8 Imperial Hotel, Tokyo, 1913–1922.

9 Designs for glassware and dinnerware, Leerdam Glassfabriek, 1929.

10 The Hillside Home School of the Allied Arts. This is the school Wright initially proposed for the vacant Hillside Home School buildings at Taliesin.

11 University of Wisconsin.

help. Enough here you see, in the work in hand to show the Frenchmen some of the things they inadvertently overlooked.

The enclosed to Douglas Haskell will tell you all of that story. I shall have to look to you for "rescue" in the end. I knew I would.

It seems the coroner's jury is sitting and both Hitchcock and Haskell are there in behalf of "Surface and Mass." The jury so far seems rather negligent of the more vital factors involved in an architecture for America. But that's the way the wind is blowing just now.

I am sending on the last article touching this subject written for the *Record* because I can see the fight coming on and I might as well as speak my mind on that subject.[12] As yet, it seems to have had no mind applied to it directly.

As for myself, I was tired of working with lame methods. My hands were sore with makeshift tools. No wonder I threw down the walls of circumstance now and then. At least my countrymen already have from me valid evidence of power? And how silly and ungrateful to brand as weakness the radiation of character from my work. Just in proportion to his force, the artist will find his work outlet for his proper character, says Emerson. But no "mannerist" could have made my varied group of buildings? I cannot hope, nor should I want to emancipate myself from my age and my country. And this quality in my work will have a higher charm, a greater value than any individual-quality could have.

The New in art is always formed out of the Old—if it is truly valid as New.

Art does exhilarate and its intoxicating aim is truly no less than the creation of man as a perfect "flower of Nature." What an excursion! As yet, however, I have never been really frivolous.

Now as a student of the mystery of form, I have found an outlet for all my energy.

No need to ask what is the mode in Paris. . . .

Nothing confounds the critic it seems, like common sense or straightforward dealing of any kind. He is taken in by surface indications of it and fails to see it as a reality beneath an exuberance.

I hope Melville is born and parturition none too devastating.

---

12 Most likely a draft for Frank Lloyd Wright, "Surface and Mass—Again!" *Architectural Record* 66 (July 1929): 92–94.

That happy look of youth you wore when last I saw you should never be impaired.

Here's a snapshot made a few days ago,—it happens to be lying on my drawing board. I send it to show you how I've wasted away since we last met,—that look of "battered up but still in the ring." Send me one of yourself to reassure me.

Tell me how all goes with you. Yesterday someone told me that truly-old I. K. Pond took exception in print to your "Sticks and Stones" because you weren't a "practicing architect."[13] What "practicing architects" know anything at all of architecture anyway,—even if they could write about it? Certainly not he.

He's a dried herring, hanging beneath the eaves of Architecture.

Don't bother,—but when the spirit moves, drop me a line. I believe in your genius and see great things ahead of you. Wish I could hurry them up,—but you are young. Stay so by means of creative work. It is the only sure way.

That book of which you spoke is now imminent. We are working on one to be published by the *Record*, another by any one of several New York publishers.[14]

I could use that promised article of yours in this connection as you suggested and be grateful.

Faithfully yours,
[signed]
Frank Lloyd Wright

---

13 Irving K. Pond (1857–1939), American architect.

14 Frank Lloyd Wright, unpublished manuscript for "Creative Matter in the Nature of Materials," a compilation of Wright's fourteen articles in the series "In the Cause of Architecture," previously published in the *Architectural Record* in 1927–1928, but much enlarged with new illustrations. See *Frank Lloyd Wright: Collected Writings, Volume 1, 1894–1930*, edited by Bruce Brooks Pfeiffer with an introduction by Kenneth Frampton (New York: Rizzoli in association with the Frank Lloyd Wright Foundation, 1992), 225–310. The second manuscript to which Wright refers may be either *An Autobiography* (London: Longmans, Green and Company, 1932) or *The Disappearing City* (New York: William Farquhor Payson, [1932]).

N.B. It has occurred to me that you might be interested to have the plates from the monograph (I have a great many loose plates which made their appearance in Germany in 1910.[15] Of course, many of the buildings were designed some years before.) In these I think you may see "Surface and Mass" prophetic. Many German architects, Menndelsohn [*sic*] among them, have told me that these things burst on their vision with an uplift in their own present direction that was tremendous.[16]

I enclose again a clipping from *Los Angeles Times*—the paper that is to the West-coast what the *New York Times* is to the East-coast,—that takes the right attitude toward this French propaganda of Lee Simonson et al.[17]

FLW:NW
Taliesin
Spring Green
Wisconsin
January 7, 1929

[pc ts&ms lmp]

15 Frank Lloyd Wright, *Ausgeführte Bauten und Entwürfe von Frank Lloyd Wright* [Berlin: Ernst Wasmuth, 1910].
16 Erich Mendelsohn (1887–1953), German architect.
17 Clipping unlocated.

[INSCRIPTION TO LEWIS MUMFORD ON LOOSE PLATE (53) OF FRANK LLOYD WRIGHT'S BURTON S. WESTCOTT RESIDENCE (SPRINGFIELD, OHIO, 1907) FROM *Ausgeführte Bauten und Entwürfe von Frank Lloyd Wright*]

Tri-dimensional Surface and Wall—(The Interior outwardly expressed). NEW. Walls are screens, roof uninterrupted planes. Offering in Europe 1910.

[ms private collection]

[SENT TO LEWIS MUMFORD, C. JANUARY 1929]

Mr. Douglas Haskell
119 West 40th Street,
New York City.

Dear Douglas Haskell:

I got a tardy look (only day before yesterday) at your *Creative Art* post-mortem.[1]

Let us be frank—

It was all expected when I telegraphed you to refrain and return material, except that the deed was better done with more painstaking sympathy. Clearly your ability to penetrate deeper than you got in this essay,—or were "allowed" to get. And, as you say I can't expect to control what is said of my work.

Your final benediction touched me and showed you not quite content.

Both yourself and Russell Hitchcock (you seem to see eye to eye) are young men in Architecture. All criticism—in any state of culture such as ours has sympathies that lie naturally in the lines and tell the truth perforce, between them.

I see we will be able to have nothing at this stage of our development that does not come with lettre de cache from France.

We are still fashionable or not sure.

I am serving an ungrateful master apparently, but shall only serve the more.

Architecture is still an art. Sophisticated Science can never take its place very long.

Were you to look in with me on the processes at work here as I write, you would see deeper than your Frenchmen, see with more a sense of Architecture than will ever be theirs. I come of a long line of Soul-Savers and would rescue yours from the French because it seems worth while.

Nature seems to have denied to them both Music and Architecture while she endowed them with "Painting" and Literature.

My best to you.

---

1 Douglas Haskell, "Organic Architecture: Frank Lloyd Wright," *Creative Art* 3 (November 1928): 51–57.

A little more and you would have penetrated to valuable matter that would have made you less satisfied with the "card-board" house.

The afternoon *Creative Art* came, I wrote a review of your article, thinking to publish it. Sort of a Selbst-Bildnis.[2]

As I wired Simonson, the corpse was risen and would talk if he would publish. He wired he would. *Creative Art* is hardly the place for me, but probably I'll go in.

Sincerely yours,

To D.H.

To make this matter as constructive as I can for "my critic"—I am sending herewith some loose plates that I happen to have (unfortunately mildewed)—copies of those that got "America" to Europe in 1910 with such effect.[3] If you will study them in the light of remarks I have attached to them, make a few tracings leaving off evidence of the third dimension, divest my surface and mass designs of the "third dimension," you will produce the "New." Cutting out the third dimension enables men who were merely architecturally "aesthetic" to build buildings as a painter makes paintings, but with little knowledge of actual construction. Two dimensions simplify their task—but Architecture insists upon three, nevertheless. Its nature will not be gainsaid. There is no possible compromise, I believe, except "on the surface."

P.S. The material sent you so promptly, photographs, I mean,—may I have it?

You promised to return it as promptly and I speak of it because it is really needed.

[cc ts flwa]

---

2 German: *Selbstbildnis*, meaning "self portrait."

3 Wright, *Ausgeführte Bauten und Entwürfe von Frank Lloyd Wright.*

Mr. Lewis Mumford
Amenia, New York

Dear Lewis Mumford:

We forgot to include the school prospectus I mentioned.

These school buildings are next to Taliesin.[1] I have owned them for ten years. I have always intended to do something of this kind with the buildings.

A telegram from *Creative Art* offering me two thousand words and six photographs to reply to Douglas Haskell's post mortem has changed my feeling about the whole matter.

I have not sent to that young man either the article or letter I sent to you but will write another. I will send it on soon. You may return those to me when you have read them.

I will forward the amended article to be published.

Faithfully yours,
FLW:NW
Taliesin
Spring Green
Wisconsin
January 10, 1929

[cc ts flwa]

---

1 Hillside Home School, Spring Green, 1902.

4002 LOCUST ST
LONG ISLAND CITY, N.Y.

18 JANUARY 1929

Dear Frank Lloyd Wright:

My warmest thanks for the portfolio: no less for a glimpse of the articles: and my hearty backing for the school! But of all this I must write later: for I am about to go off to Denver for a series of lectures at the Art Museum—leaving behind me, you can imagine with what feelings, a household almost prostrated with illness.

Ever yours,
[signed]
Lewis Mumford

[ms flwa]

LLOYD WRIGHT[1]
LOS ANGELES, CALIFORNIA
858 DOHENY DRIVE
PHONE OX 7608

FEBRUARY 1, 1929

My Dear Lewis Mumford :

Have just read your discourse on Decore, or "The rigors and rigidities of the machine economy made tolerable "by" the surplus left over for the personal arts."[2]

Apparently in your opinion, machine economy, of necessity is intolerable and does not permit an expression of personality (personal character).

It is daily demonstrated here now, and for some time past, that the economies of the machine need neither be rigid, frigid, or intolerable, nor lacking in opportunity for personal expression.

That you do not yet realize it, indicates the shortness of your travels into this field you attempt to critisize [*sic*] so meticulously in spots.

And speaking of meticulous criticism, accuracy and meticulous consideration are sadly lacking in your summation of "this field," which, by the way, Gropius and Le Corbusier have, but lately and most obviously "joined," and with the callow enthusiasm of the green horn, loudly and superficially proclaimed.

It is clear that you have not practised the art you critisize.

"There can be no honest and virile design until the artist decides for himself which side he is on."

Sincerely yours.
[signed]
Lloyd Wright

[pc ts&ms lmp]

---

1 Frank Lloyd Wright, Jr., known as Lloyd Wright (1890–1978), American architect and oldest son of Frank Lloyd Wright.

2 Lewis Mumford, "The Economics of Contemporary Decoration," *Creative Art* 4 (January 1929): 19–22.

4002 LOCUST STREET
LONG ISLAND CITY, N.Y.

12 MAY 1929

Dear Frank Lloyd Wright:

Your wrote me last January, just as I was on the eve of starting out for a course of lectures in Denver: my little child was ill then, and I was stopped at Chicago by a sore throat and compelled to turn back: and from that time right on to the middle of April life was pretty stormy and black; for my little boy had a double mastoid and was within a hairs breadth, literally of passing out: and the strain of his long illness and slow recovery left a scar on the whole household: so that I did not do a stroke of work until the end of March.[1] We are all beginning to thrive again: but if I had sent you a snapshot of me a few months ago you would, perhaps have had a little difficulty in recognizing it. That review of Hitchcock's monograph, in the April *Record*, was written, fortunately, last autumn: but all the things that I promised myself to do during the winter have fallen by the wayside; and I must go back and pick them up.[2] My present task is to do a short article on Modern Architecture 1850—to date, for the new *Encyclopedia of Social Sciences*: a hard thing to compass in a few thousand words.[3] I had a good week in Madison at the end of April; but was disappointed to learn that you were in Arizona, for, had you been home, I should have played hookey for an afternoon. Meiklejohn's Experimental College, where I lectured and had endless discussions, is the real thing: a complete break with cram and drill and routine.[4] The experience at first throws the students off their feet: it is a shocking change for them: but when they get back again they are on the way to knowing what an education and intellectual responsibility are. The university is hostile to Meiklejohn: for his methods, if successful, would rout them out of all their old habits: but

1 Geddes Mumford (1925–1944), son of Lewis and Sophia Mumford (1899–1997).

2 Lewis Mumford, review of *Frank Lloyd Wright*, by Henry-Russell Hitchcock, Jr., *Architectural Record* 65 (April 1929): 414–416.

3 Lewis Mumford, "Architecture: Since the Renaissance," in *Encyclopedia of the Social Sciences* II (New York: Macmillan Co., 1930): 172–175.

4 Alexander Meiklejohn (1872–1964), educator; Chairman, Experimental College, University of Wisconsin, Madison.

this college is the nucleus for new education, and I mourned that it was in old Peabody's buildings, and not in one of yours, that its physical life is carried on.[5] My lectures went fairly well; and I have a notion that if your own school plans are in need of help at the University, my word would count for more now than it would have last January! Did you hear about my lecture at the Civic Club in Madison, on the New Spirit in Architecture? One of the papers, I am told, featured what I said about you: but I didn't see the report. I know I scandalized the good ladies: they waited patiently to be told what a marvelous Capitol and Campus they had—and they waited. It was one of the best lectures I have ever given; and I learned later that they were furious about it. I gave a similar lecture in Chicago, in the old Harold McCormick house; but that went better: it was more intimate: and the chamber of horrors in which I spoke was very effective for illustration; indeed, a few of the ladies there were living in modern houses, or knew other people who did![6] In Chicago, I lectured to Lovett's classes in the arts, and had a jolly time generally. Shall you be in New York soon? I am eager to see you. The news of your new work delights me, and I should like to see that, too. Financially, the Melville has set me on my feet, for it was taken over by the Literary Guild, just in time to meet the three thousand dollars worth of doctor's bills and nursing expenses that toppled on our heads! Also, the last proof of my "arrival" has come with the Melville: all sorts of people, who had been storing their bile and vindictiveness for the last few years, have come out in the open and turned these loose on me! I winced at the first blow or two: for it puzzled me at first: but when I realized that the animus was not directed against my work—the Melville is my best so far—but against me, and against me for having "arrived," my perturbation turned into a grin. The other day I happened upon the reviews of my first book, *The Story of Utopias*, a promising but very immature book, done at twenty-six: they were all one paean of praise; even the conservative critics were sweet in their disparagement.[7] Now, it happens, I am big enough to serve as a symbol or a target: hence the bullets. Good: I can fight, too, if the time has arrived for fighting. I daresay you have been through all

5 Arthur Peabody (1858–1942), American architect.

6 Cudell and Blumenthal, McCormick Residence (demolished), Chicago, 1875–1879.

7 Lewis Mumford, *The Story of Utopias* (New York: Boni and Liveright, 1922).

this more than once: but literary warfare is a little more open than it is in the other professions, and one realizes more quickly what is happening, and who is making it happen.

Warm greetings and good wishes
[signed]
Lewis Mumford

[ts flwa]

Mr. Lewis Mumford
Amenia, New York

Dear Lewis Mumford:

What a shame that you've been to Madison near my Wisconsin home while I've been out here in Arizona with the rattlesnakes, scorpions, tarantulas, et al,—but busy on a really important work.

A clipping reaches me that tells me of your message to the Badgers in my "Old Home Town" and Alma Mater, too.[1] And better still Lawrence Kocher sends me the *Record* for April with your review in it.[2]

That piece of work seems to me a solid piece of constructive criticism. One that will go far at this time to squarely meet an issue rendered equivocal by Hitchcock and Haskell, who should have known better than they knew.

You put the case so solidly on its base that there is little room for the much-argument that will undoubtedly follow. Your head seems pretty well set on a pair of good shoulders and your heart in the right place,—your own country.

I can't thank you enough. All personal gratification aside, you are the one best asset the country has to awaken her to her good and proper work.

More power to you,—and it is coming. My son Lloyd in Los Angeles read your article in *Creative Arts* [*sic*] and misapprehending you, wrote you a letter with a copy to me. He went off half-cocked. I was sorry he wrote the letter and he deserves more than the language of that epistle might indicate. You'll meet him one day and help to iron him out.

We are going to Taliesin soon and it would be swell if you and Mrs. Mumford and the little Mumfords could come out to one of our cottages there for a summer-time in that lovely Southern Wisconsin region.[3]

A note from Wijdefeld[4] [*sic*] in Holland says he is ready and anxious

---

1 University of Wisconsin, which Wright attended in 1886.

2 Alfred Lawrence Kocher (1886–1969), architect, educator and editor at *Architectural Record*.

3 Sophia Mumford, née Wittenberg (1899–1997), American editor and wife of Lewis Mumford.

4 Hendricus Theodorus Wijdeveld (1885–1987), Dutch architect, writer, and educator.

to come too and get into the work of the "international school" of the Fine-Arts.[5]

More of all this when I return. Only let me know where to find you by kindly dropping a note to the Spring Green Address.

Faithfully yours,
[signed]
Frank Lloyd Wright
FLW:NW
Chandler
Arizona
May 12, 1929

[pc ts lmp]

---

5 A reference to the evolving concept for Wright's proposed school.

AMENIA
NEW YORK

22 JULY 1929

Dear Frank Lloyd Wright:

I can't account for my remissness in answering the good letter you wrote in May, except by the fact that, when the tension of the winter at last relaxed—and it was for me the worst winter I've had to weather—I slumped more than usual, and in that state I couldn't bear to write to you. Six weeks of tramping and swimming up here have changed both Sophie and me and our little boy: and I can face the world now with a little of my old jauntiness. I am leaving at the end of this week to give a series of five lectures in Geneva: from which point I hope to go directly into Holland, in order, among other things, to see what your work looks like when it has undergone a sea-change and fermented in foreign minds.[1] A letter from Hitchcock informs me that he has become somewhat disillusioned with Le Corbusier: so if I should see him in passing, I shall wrestle with him and see what I can do with him! I shall be back here around the end of September; and if you make another visit to the East please tell me: but better let me know at my city address, 4002 Locust Street, Long Island City. Have you done any houses other than those whose photographs I have, lately? Walter Curt Behrendt, a friend of mine who used to edit *Die Form*, is getting out a book on the modern house and wants American examples.[2] He has, however, perhaps written to you personally. What about your son's work? Can I get some photos of it for Behrendt? I have lost Lloyd Wright's address or I would write him personally.

What is happening to your International School project? I shall try to see Wijdeveld when I am in Amsterdam; and if you can think of anyone else whom it would be well to have a talk with, or whose work I ought to know, please drop me a line when you get this to:

---

1 Geneva, Switzerland, where Mumford lectured at the International Summer School in 1925 and 1929.

2 Walter Curt Behrendt (1884–1945), German writer and editor; this work was evidently not published.

Hotel Mirabeau, Geneva, Switzerland.

My head is now humming with a half dozen books that I want to write; and I am waiting for the time when one of them will temporarily slay all the rest and permit me to go to work. In the meanwhile, I have done a few sociological papers for *Architecture*, and am mulling over some things to give to Kocher. This is a good time to be living: there is a ferment at work all over, and as I turn from one field to another, I can recognize, in each, a handful of spirits whose work, when combined with similar attitudes and projects and deeds in other groups, will revolutionize both the inner and the outer man. It is part of my business, I think, to make these groups more fully acquainted with each other, and to permit them to recognize and collect their united forces. Hence my specialism is to keep out of specialties.

Forgive this long silence and let me know how you prosper.

Devotedly yours,
[signed]
Lewis Mumford

[ts flwa]

Mr. Lewis Mumford
Hotel Mirabeau
Geneva, Switzerland

My dear Lewis Mumford:

Either you overlooked my earnest invitation to bring Mrs. Mumford and the little Mumford,—I don't know whether I should write the word singular or plural,—to Taliesin for a visit. Of course Europe is a great deal better and I am glad you are foot-loose for a time. No doubt you need the freshening up after so much hard work. I imagine you do work hard. You have the signs and symptoms of energy about you. I think you might like this old place,—my old farm house,—and it would certainly open its arms to receive you and try to make your stay memorable.

We are interested in several projects that would interest you. I won't drag them in now.

I have sent for your books, anxious to read your "Melville." I have heard a number of flattering comments on that work. And I was glad to learn that you are learning to place the opposition for what it is worth.

Any man will learn as much from his enemies as from his friends. They keep him in fighting trim. Adverse criticism, when it is sincere,—which unfortunately it seldom is,—being usually either envious or politic, is good. You have the right attitude toward it.

Here's hoping you find true recreation this summer.

I don't know anybody in Europe in whom I am particularly interested. There is Oud, Widjeveld, Perret, Stevens, Corbusier, et al., Bruno Taut, Gropius, Mendelsohn, Dudok and the men of Holland.[1] But none the less, there are many younger men coming up in between of great interest if we knew who they were. Few of these men seem to me to have grasped anything profound but are all tremendously skillful, talented, and artistic and all moving with good direction, or at least the proper sense of it. When you take the work of these men in

1 J. J. P. Oud (1890–1963), Dutch architect and planner; Auguste Perret (1874–1954), French architect; Robert Mallet-Stevens (1886–1945), French architect and designer; Bruno Taut (1880–1938), German architect and theorist; Willem Marinus Dudok (1884–1974), Dutch architect.

the aggregate its content is more shallow than it should be and its form too much iteration and reiteration.

I wonder how they will like the article in the July *Record*, printed in the notes and comments in the rear of the magazine under the caption "Surface and Mass,—Again."[2] I am afraid they won't like it much. But saying it won't hurt them. It may help some of them.

When you return, drop me a note. We expect to be at Taliesin until November first this colorful fall. Perhaps we could meet somewhere for a talk, preferably here of course.

Faithfully yours,
FLlW:NW
Taliesin
Spring Green
Wisconsin
August 6, 1929

[cc ts&ms flwa]

2 Frank Lloyd Wright, "Surface and Mass—Again!" *Architectural Record* 66 (July 1929): 92–94.

Mr Lewis Mumford
Amenia, New York

My dear Lewis Mumford:

I've been wondering if you've forgotten the Mendelsohn or only are just busy as the happy consequence of a well-deserved success.[1]

Since seeing you I've read "The Golden Day" and Melville, winding up with "Moby Dick."[2] I had a good time and feel I know you quite well now. Your Melville is quite worthy [of] Moby Dick himself. A very fine study—yours—in that work.

I wish I, myself, could write. As it is, I am to be "lecturer." Princeton asks me to come and deliver the course this coming May and ask[s] to publish.[3] Inasmuch as I shall receive money for the lectures I close my "amateurship." Yes, now I am a "lecturer." "Singularly doomed to what we execrate and writhe to shun." I've saved the day however, by making the seventh an Exhibition of my recent work.[4]

We are designing and setting it up here with an idea of letting it leave Princeton on tour of the U.S.A. We are giving it careful attention, making models as well as drawings using fresh old material, as well. You know, Lewis, I am sorry I called poor Hitchcock a fool and am writing to take back a swipe at his latest book[;] I wrote it for the *Record*.[5]

Why should I try to hurt him? He is at least sincere. What if he doesn't know? He may learn. Anyhow, I can't strike the blow. It is not to my taste.

I hope you are as well as you looked the last time I saw you, and mean to come with your wife and child to see us and ours—some day this spring?

---

1 Erich Mendelsohn, "Frank Lloyd Wright und seine historische Bedeutung," *Das Neue Berlin* 4 (September 1929): 180–181.

2 Lewis Mumford, *The Golden Day: A Study of American Experience and Culture* (New York: Boni and Liveright, 1926).

3 Princeton University, where Wright lectured in spring 1930; later published as Frank Lloyd Wright, *Modern Architecture, Being the Kahn Lectures for 1930* (Princeton, New Jersey: Princeton University Press, 1931).

4 Wright organized a large exhibition for Princeton University, which subsequently toured the United States, including New York City, and Holland, Belgium, and Germany in 1930–1931.

Can't you look ahead far enough now to say when you can all come for a week? You can work here you know!

Faithfully,
[signed]
Frank Lloyd Wright
Taliesin
Spring Green
Wisconsin
December 17—1930
[1929, corrected date]

[pc ts&ms lmp]

1930

Wright's practice is devastated by the stock market crash of October 1929, but his reputation is bolstered by an invitation to lecture at Princeton University in spring 1930, where he also mounts an exhibition of his work that will subsequently travel to several venues in the United States and Europe. In July, Wright and Mumford are reunited at a special dinner in honor of Wright thrown by the Architectural League of New York, further evidence of Wright's increased recognition by the East Coast "establishment." Mention is made in their letters of the upcoming 1933 World's Fair in Chicago, in which Wright has not yet been invited to participate. Mumford, at work on a new history of the arts in late-nineteenth-century America, asks Wright to clarify his relationship with his mentor, Louis Sullivan.

LEWIS MUMFORD
4002 LOCUST STREET
LONG ISLAND CITY, N.Y.

11 MARCH 1930

Dear Frank Lloyd Wright:

I have been both busy & gay all winter—up to this week when, with the ailments of Job plaguing me, I suddenly find myself with "leisure." This is not the right sort of time to do letters in: but it is now or never! I am glad you are going to Princeton; someone must be trying to break loose there, and you can at least saw off the ball & chain for him. As for your exhibition, you ought to deposit it in our midst at least half a year before letting it go on tour: we need a human antidote to the inspired madness of Buckminster Fuller; & even Hitchcock may let his eyes convert him to what his intelligence rejects![1] Forgive me for turning the Mendelsohn article back without a proper translation: the gist of it is that you are the father of modern form. In creating modern architecture, Olbrich worked from steel construction: you used the static compositions of old materials, wood & stone, & the new pressed concrete.[2] Both processes were revolutionary & both were necessary. Today both are being united in a common platform, as the foundation for modern architecture. You already have an evolutionary value & no longer a comparative value for today. Your mastery is indisputable. This is rough: but the core of it. I am pleased that you have read *Melville*. After the hell of my last year I appreciate the poor devil's ailings better than I did when I wrote the biography.

Warmly yours,
[signed]
LM

[ms flwa]

1 Richard Buckminster Fuller (1895–1983), American architect, engineer, designer, theorist, and writer.
2 Joseph Maria Olbrich (1867–1908), Austrian architect.

Mr. Lewis Mumford
4002 Locust St
Long Island City
New York

My Dear Lewis:

Herewith a little "hors-d'oeuvre" for the Princeton Lectures available to all the first evening.[1] As you will see by this, our hat is "in the ring."

You passed by in silence my cordial invitation to "Taliesin" this Spring, why?

Sincerely,
Frank Lloyd Wright
Taliesin
Spring Green
Wisconsin
April the fourteenth
nineteen thirty

[cc ts flwa]

---

1 Text for Wright's first Princeton lecture, "Machinery, Materials, and Men."

4002 LOCUST STREET
LONG ISLAND CITY, N.Y.

19 APRIL 1930

Dear Frank Lloyd Wright:

Thanks for your brave and beautiful manifesto: it adds to my treasures! When do the lectures come off? I know more than one youngster in New York who'd like to make the pilgrimage to Princeton to hear you.

It wasn't churlishness that made me omit to respond to your invitation. I could scarcely say No without mentioning the round of plagues and miseries that have been at us again this spring: and since I was still in the midst of them at the time I said nothing. I am better now, and little Geddes has had his tonsils taken out just now, and I myself will follow his example in a fortnight or so—and then it will be time to get back to my book and settle down for the summer in the country.[1] Better luck next year! I have been asked to spend the spring term at Ohio State; and if I accept, one more jump would bring us at your door.

Please let me see you if you have time when you're in New York. If I am able I'll run out to Princeton.

Ever warmly
[signed]
Lewis

[ts flwa]

1 Either a reference to Lewis Mumford, *The Brown Decades: A Study of the Arts in America, 1865–1895* (New York: Harcourt, Brace and Company, 1931) or Lewis Mumford, "Form and Personality/Form and Civilization," unpublished typescript that became the basis for The Renewal of Life series, Lewis Mumford Papers (hereafter lmp), Annenbery Rare Book and Manuscript Library, University of Pennsylvania, Philadelphia, Pennsylvania.

[C. JUNE, 1930]

Lewis Mumford
Long Island
New York

My dear Lewis:

I looked all over the place for you without success just before we sat down to dinner and got no chance to talk with you the night of the "League" to thank you for your excellent talk at the table.[1] The others were meant to be "high wide and handsome" and somewhat were, but you said the thing to be said, as you usually do.

I can think of little else very well worth remembering except the spectacle of our hard-boiled New Yorkers coming across for our little home-made show.[2]

I am again indebted to you for your vision and courage. Before long I should begin to "come back to you." At Princeton I was asked on several different occasions—what do you think of Lewis Mumford[?] (Showing you were on their minds out there[.]) My answer was, "The most valuable critic our country has—a mind of Emersonian quality,—with true creative power." Said my hostess one evening, "But don't you think the young man too "cock sure"? "Not of anything he doesn't actually grasp," I said.

On the other hand, there was no serious consideration of cocksure Hitchcock. Said Forsythe (Chair of Archaeology)[,] "If Hitchcock wrote his opinions without giving illustrations he might receive some thoughtless credence—but every time he shows a picture he shows himself up."[3] The students within hearing laughed their acquiescence. The twigs incline to the direction of the wind? Every innovation brings a flood of incompetent criticism. The New York boys backed up their enthusiasm by refusing to let me pay for my expenses to and from New York or for entertainment while there or for any costs in connection with the show at all. Moreover, they say to me there is a genuine

---

1 Architectural League of New York.

2 Exhibition of Wright's work that originated at Princeton University and moved to the Architectural League of New York, spring 1930.

3 George Howard Forsyth (1901–1991), American archaeologist and educator.

Frank Lloyd Wright at his desk, Taliesin, Spring Green, Wisconsin, c. 1924. Frank Lloyd Wright Archives, 6004.0014.

Lewis Mumford, c. 1938. Estate of Lewis and Sophia Mumford.

Olgivanna Lloyd Wright and Iovanna Wright, Minneapolis, 1926. Frank Lloyd Wright Archives, 6401.0006.

IOVANNA
MARRIED AUGUST 25
RANCHO SANTA
FE CALIFORNIA
OLGA IVANOVNA
DAUGHTER OF
IVAN LAZOVICH AND
MILITZA MILAN OF
CETTINJE MONTENEGRO
TO FRANK LLOYD WRIGHT
SON OF ANNA LLOYD-JONES
AND WILLIAM CARY WRIGHT
TALIESIN WISCONSIN 1928

Wedding announcement of Frank Lloyd Wright and Olga Ivanovna Lazovich, August 26, 1928. Frank Lloyd Wright Archives, 2803.002.

Taliesin West, Scottsdale, Arizona, 1937. View toward drafting room, 1946. Photograph by Maynard Parker. Frank Lloyd Wright Archives, 3803.0006.

Frank Lloyd Wright and Olgivanna Lloyd Wright at Taliesin, 1958. Photograph by Bruce Brooks Pfeiffer. Frank Lloyd Wright Archives, 6204.0008.

Taliesin, Spring Green, Wisconsin, 1925. Exterior view, 1937. Photograph by Hedrich-Blessing. Chicago Historical Society; Frank Lloyd Wright Archives, 2501.0235.

Geddes, Alison, and Sophia Mumford, Palo Alto, California, 1943. Estate of Lewis and Sophia Mumford.

Mumford Residence, Leedsville, near Amenia, New York, c. 1955. Estate of Lewis and Sophia Mumford.

Lewis and Sophia Mumford, Ledbury, England, July 1957. Estate of Lewis and Sophia Mumford.

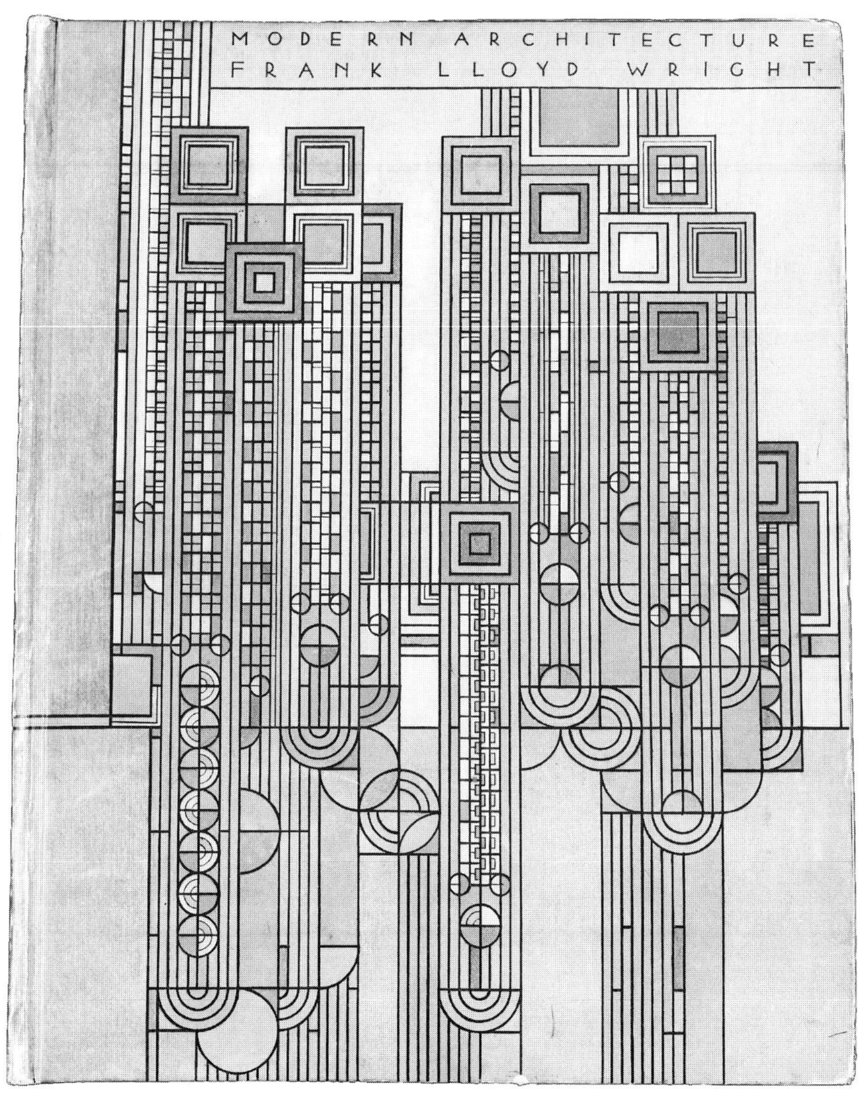

Frank Lloyd Wright, cover of *Modern Architecture, Being the Kahn Lectures for 1930*, Princeton University Press, 1931. Frank Lloyd Wright Archives, 7001.0023.

desire on their part to take me "in" on the Chicago fair in some way where I can be really useful.[4] What that way is I don't know yet. Corbett, Walker, Hood, and Kahn gave me this much advance notice.[5] But please understand my dear Lewis, I am really uncomfortable with this "recognition." Am I really losing my power and so they are no longer afraid of me? I shall have to go carefully from now on—not recklessly as before. Doing a "Lindberg" in architecture is more fun in itself than any of its consequences can ever be.[6]

Have heard nothing from Scribners about the "book"—but soon I suppose.[7]

In a year from now my dear man! Meantime—"all I can."

Faithfully,
[signed]
Frank Lloyd Wright
Taliesin
Spring Green
Wisconsin

[pc ts&ms lmp]

4 A reference to the upcoming 1933 Century of Progress Exposition (1933 World's Fair) in Chicago.
5 American architects, Harvey W. Corbett (1873–1954), Ralph T. Walker (1889–1973), Raymond M. Hood (1881–1934), and Ely-Jacques Kahn (1884–1972).
6 A reference to Charles Lindbergh's 1927 transatlantic flight.
7 Frank Lloyd Wright, unpublished manuscript for "Creative Matter in the Nature of Materials."

AMENIA, NEW YORK

1 JULY 1930

Dear Frank Lloyd Wright:

It was good to hear from you; but the memory of that dinner makes me grit my teeth and cuss. Those boys all meant to do the right thing, I have no doubt: they knew that they owed you a debt and that the world owed you a debt, too: at bottom, they realized that they were honoring themselves for posterity by holding a banquet in your honor. But when the time came for them to speak up, their original intention was smothered over in their vanity and what was even worse[,] their necessity for self-justification: and they never properly got around to you. If only I had spoken last! Anticipating that the others would do something more than confess and apologize and beat around the bush, and not wishing to leave all other eulogies in position of being anti-climaxes, I was very reserved in my remarks: and each fresh speech of theirs made me regret that reserve. How bamboozled they all are by their own "success." They can really think of nothing else. They respect you and envy you because you have had a different kind of success: but they were as unable to express the first as they were impotent to conceal the second. I saw the same miserly attitude in another dinner of honor, that to Waldo Frank:[1] and I swear that I will never attend another one in America, even though it be given to me! A lot of jackals with a lion in their midst! (Oh: I know that their hearts are in the right place, and they don't mean to be offensive: but doubtless the jackal can say the same thing.) The younger men, as you doubtless know, are much closer to you. One of them, Henry Churchill, is going to make a trip to Chicago.[2] He has done some good work and is capable of doing better. I could see that he was much impressed by you; and he asked me if I would give him an introduction to you. Please consider this the introduction. He is worth any time you may be able to spare him; and though he has gone fairly far, he is still young enough to be influenced from within. The day of your power is just beginning.

1 Waldo David Frank (1889–1967), American writer.

2 Henry S. Churchill (1893–1962), American writer.

I salute you at the beginning of a great career!!!

I am warmed about what you say of L.M.: but the remarks of your hostess about my cock-sureness makes me prick up my ears. One can never get a true picture of one-self, or at all events, the sort of picture that would satisfy an outsider: and this is one of the vices I had never even suspected. On reflection, I think I know what she means: a cock-sureness in matters of faith, not in matters of fact: the inner conviction. That always seems a shaky scaffold to the people who don't see the building behind it. Good heavens: I am obsessed rather by the persistence of my diffidence; and am resolved to speak louder and more emphatically!

Sophie is now in Europe and Geddes and I are living alone in this farmhouse; and for the present doing very nicely thank you.[3] The first rough draft of my book is done, and, since the chapter on Building more or less leads up to you, I have one or two questions to ask you.[4] How far were you hindered by Sullivan's example? How much of him did you have to throw overboard? Did you do this consciously or unconsciously? Which of your buildings represents to you the climax of your work—if any single building so stands out?. . . This philosophy of the arts is the toughest problem I've set myself yet, and I am afraid there'll be snow on the ground before I've even half done with it. Then I shall go on a bust and write poetry again and finish a play!

Affectionately yours
[signed]
Lewis

[ts flwa]

3 Mumford family summer residence in Leedsville, near Amenia, New York; after 1936, it became the family's permanent residence.

4 Mumford, *The Brown Decades*.

Dear Lewis

Would you like to come to Wisconsin second semester, say Feb. 1st for a week,—similar to "before"[?][1]

You made many friends there who would like to hear you again.

Let me know at your earliest convenience. I am asked to "feel you out"!

Dr. Guthrie—(St. Marks in the Bouwerie)—said "Mumford was the star of your occasion—.[2] He looked the knight-errant of ideas, too. I'm going to have him down to the church,—a symposium—. He made a great impression upon me." Yes, I said, but don't expect him unless you've got $50.00 to pay him for fifteen minutes. All right, said he, fair enough!

Faithfully
[signed]
Frank Lloyd Wright
Taliesin
July 4th
1930

[pc ts&ms lmp]

---

1 University of Wisconsin.

2 William Norman Guthrie (1868–1944), American clergyman and client of Frank Lloyd Wright.

Mr. Lewis Mumford
Long Island
New York

My Dear Lewis

I understand your rage. But do not expect too much, too soon.

Recollect how far they had to go—on how little!

Your letter cheers me. The quality of youth and fire in you is tonic and bracing.

No, we are not through yet. Between us I believe there is much to be accomplished—A crusade. You know.

And the merely religious ones now History, seem like child's make-believe in comparison.

This will be Man conquering his Machine—his mind breaking prison, and going free.

The "Protestants" are already invading the field—But let's keep this cause Catholic in the finest sense of the word.

"Affirmation"! Every move and utterance universal in application. No time wasted in or on mere protest. Protestants are useful—they have never been beautiful.

To answer your questions . . .

1. Helped rather than hindered by Sullivan—because—though pupil, I think I was never his disciple. (It is the disciple who is hindered by his master.) Sullivan is on record as gratefully acknowledging this.

2. We had many differences, some marked, early in our relationship. For instance, admiring his ornament I craved the architectural, geometric element at first so lacking in that ornament, and injected it where ever I had opportunity. The ideal was integral ornament but the ornament seldom achieved that ideal except in itself.

3. Sullivan cared nothing for materials as qualifying design. All were alike—grist for his mill. Perhaps my delight in the square-cut and the rectilinear were, in some small degree, reaction from too sensuous fluctuation and flutter of surface—Sullivan's ebullient-efflorescence. In the Winslow House (my first really independent work in 1892–93) you may see Sullivan in the frieze—you see him nowhere else.[1]

---

1 William H. Winslow Residence, River Forest, Illinois, 1893.

To me, (although implicit in all I did from the first), the Larkin-Building made definitely the negation now engaging Le Corbusier et al. Unity Temple went a step further on from that negation to affirmation.[2] The Coonley House—a step further still.[3] There was a conscious striving for organic-simplicity in my work (from the first moment I began on my own) which I did not owe to anyone, I believe.[4] I am enclosing a post-mortem held by myself at Princeton on the conscious phases of that early effort.[5] The word "plastic" Sullivan used in relation to his ornament—in the ornament itself he often realized it. That quality got into his buildings but seldom.

4. No building as "climax." All are quite complete in themselves but index to those yet to come nearer to fulfillment. There seems to me a very consistent quality in them all—as expressions—in varying materials under changing conditions,—the "plastic ideal" of an organic architecture. Every building I have built bears witness in some way to the working of that ideal—and from first to last. Of course I've more "data" now (the fruit of experience)—more science. Future buildings will be sure to be more direct and more complete synthesis of the same ideal.

Here's hoping!

Kindly return the manuscript as it is the original and the copy is at Princeton.

Guthrie and wife have just been at Taliesin for a week. He's a good ballyhoo for you—. He took your *Golden Day* and *Melville* with him.

He has a crazy streak in him but he is capable of a lot of good work. Let him cultivate your acquaintance which he is set upon doing.

---

2 Unity Temple, Oak Park, Illinois, 1905.

3 Avery Coonley Residence, Riverside, Illinois, 1907.

4 Wright first defined the term "organic" in 1914 to describe his preferred design process in which the desired form would emerge naturally from the required function of the building, as distinguished from a form that would be applied merely from without. He began using the term with greater frequency in the 1930s to separate his architecture from works by his European and American peers. See Frank Lloyd Wright, "In the Cause of Architecture: Second Paper," *Architectural Record* 35 (May 1914): 405–413. Reprinted in *Frank Lloyd Wright: Collected Writings, Volume 1, 1884–1930*, 126–137.

5 Wright, manuscript for *Modern Architecture*.

Affectionately,
[signed]
Frank Lloyd Wright
Taliesin
July 7th
1930

[pc ts&ms lmp]

AMENIA, N.Y.

24 AUGUST 1930

Dear FLW:

Forgive my long delay in sending you back this chapter: there were so many important things in it that I wanted it by me while I was writing my section on architecture in my new book—a book that drags a little, alas! partly because there is much to say, and no one has yet shown me how to say it.[1] But Sophie came back from Europe a few weeks ago, beautiful & confident & quite her old—that is, youthful—self. So I am back at work again with something like my old energy & joie de vivre. Thank heaven for that: I am nothing if not a healthy writer, and I never sit down to my desk unless I am in top form & could tramp on the hills or spade a garden with equal vigor. Churchill writes me that he had a glorious time with you & found Taliesin the summit of his architectural dreams. I envy him. I liked Woolcott's [*sic*] article on you, and if I hadn't accidentally done a series of obituaries in the *New Republic* lately, I'd be tempted to echo it there![2]

Affectionately yours,
[signed]
Lewis

[ms flwa]

---

1 Mumford, *The Brown Decades*.

2 Alexander Woollcott (1887–1943), writer, editor, and critic; Alexander Woollcott, "The Prodigal Father," *New Yorker* 6 (19 July 1930): 22–25. A reference to an obituary by Mumford of his British colleague, Victor Branford; see Lewis Mumford, "Victor Branford," *New Republic* 64 (27 August 1930): 43–44. Mumford may also be referring to a biographical essay in press about his long-deceased American colleague, Randolph Bourne; see Lewis Mumford, "The Image of Randolph Bourne," *New Republic* 64 (24 September 1930): 151–152.

1931

The letters from the first half of the year are dominated by a discussion of the 1933 Chicago World's Fair. In a January article for the *New Republic*, Mumford unleashes a withering attack on the fair's organizing committee. The controversy culminates with a lecture by Wright at New York's Town Hall in February, at which occasion Mumford rises to the architect's defense. This affair is soon eclipsed by news of an upcoming exhibition on modern architecture to be co-curated by Henry-Russell Hitchcock, Jr. and Philip Johnson at the Museum of Modern Art. Both Wright and Mumford are wary of the exhibition's emphasis on European architects and their machine-inspired aesthetics, but Wright eventually agrees to be a part of it.

In June, both men are asked to comment on the recently unveiled plans for Rockefeller Center, or "Radio City," as the project is known at the outset. As one of the few major developments to be launched as the Depression worsens, Rockefeller Center generates great excitement in the press, but Mumford, writing for the *New Yorker*, and Wright, for the *New York Evening Post*, each find its scale to be overwhelming and its design uninspired. Wright continues to refine his proposal for a school in the latter part of the year. Mumford is hired by the *New Yorker* as its regular architecture critic.

Mr. Lewis Mumford,
4112 Gosman Ave.,
Long Island City,
N.Y.

Dear Lewis:

I intend to keep on the good side of you—if I can. That fist of yours pack[s] an awful wallop—. Oh Boy; I can hear the impact of that article in the *New Republic* on New York "spacemaker's for rent"—clear out on this lonely hill.[1]

If I could write like you—I might put the cause of Modern Architecture over single-handed.

I am to be in New York the week beginning February 23rd, and hope to see something of you and tell you how I feel about the whole business—.

Faithfully,
Frank Lloyd Wright,
Taliesin,
Spring Green,
Wisc.
Jan. 24, 1931.

[cc ts flwa]

1 Lewis Mumford, "Two Chicago Fairs," *New Republic* 65 (21 January 1931): 271–272.

Mr. Lewis Mumford,
4112 Gosman Ave.,
Long Island City,
N.Y.

Dear Lewis:

I thought it best before sailing into the Fair set-up—to serve Notice.[1] This is it,—so I hope to see you in New York.

Sincerely yours,
Frank Lloyd Wright,
Taliesin,
Spring Green,
Wisconsin,
February, 17, 1931.

[cc ts flwa]

---

1 Frank Lloyd Wright, lecture concerning the 1933 Century of Progress Exposition given before the American Union of Decorative Artists and Craftsmen (AUDAC), Town Hall, New York, 26 February 1931.

[RETYPED COPY SENT TO LEWIS MUMFORD]
(COPY OF LETTER SENT TO RAYMOND HOOD)

Mr. Raymond Hood,
Architect,
American Radiator Building,
West 40th Street,
New York City.

My dear Ray Hood:

A situation I don't like at all is growing up around my "unemployment" in connection with the Chicago Fair. The disagreeable feature of the situation arises from the false assumption that the Fair is a public concern and representative of the country,—which I'm sure from what you've said and what I've heard otherwise—is a mistake. It is not and is not intended to be. All I know directly about the situation is what you told me yourself. You said I was to do a building at the Fair,—and later I made a suggestion in that connection to which you replied in a note concerned also with other matters, asking me to "leave it all to you." Of course, I have no other choice. It is not up to me in any way as I see it. As you gave me to understand it the present Architects got the Job direct from Dawes—and being pretty well satisfied with each other—feel it entirely within their rights to do the Job themselves as they best can.[1]

The private nature of the enterprise not being generally understood,—of course I've heard incessant complaints, accusations by the hundreds of injustice etc. etc.—and from all over the country. "The Nation" broke into print,—more recently the "New Republic" but with no instigation from me.[2] Now I'm asked to attend a public meeting on the subject to which the press is to be invited in New York in a couple of weeks.

I can't really see why the matter has been allowed to become so damned important either way—either by your committee or by my friends. But so it seems to be. Nor do I see that all this, once the Fair is

1 Rufus Cutler Dawes (1867–1940), president of board of trustees, 1933 Century of Progress Exposition.

2 Douglas Haskell, "Frank L. Wright and the Chicago Fair," *Nation* 131 (3 December 1930): 605; Mumford, "Two Chicago Fairs."

confessed as a private enterprise, gets to you fellows in any way where you live. But until that is plain it does put me in an awkward situation, which I don't like at all, and which I propose to end in no uncertain terms at the proposed meeting.

Of course if the Fair aims to be representative of Modern Architecture the situation is too small and mean for a man like yourself. . . . I don't know the others except as I met Walker and Corbett at the League Dinner. I can only see and say that the Fair,—being a private and personal affair and made peculiar to yourselves by Dawes,—I can see no reason why if you want to do it yourselves since you got the drop of the hat, you shouldn't run your race against time or whatever it is you choose to run against—. And if you feel I would spoil your party—(it is noised around you do feel that way)—why that is your affair and they can figure it out. I am not interested. But if the Fair shows itself as Modern Architecture and is to be sold as such to the American Public in which I do have a stake—equal at least to your own recent one,—in that connection,—then only over my dead body, say I.

There has been some such attempt on Dr. Corbett's part in the past that got to me and raised the ruff on my neck some—. But never mind until we get to that. What I want you to do, Ray, if you can, is to get permission to write me a letter in this connection that I can use at the meeting to put myself fairly and squarely where I belong and end the discussion once and for all. I don't know of anything in my career that has been so insulting to me as an Architect or to yourselves as well as the present impasse is becoming because of this misapprehension as to the Nature of the Fair as an enterprise.

Let me have this straight . . . You don't need me in the Fair you are doing for Dawes and I don't need the Fair in that connection either.

I claim your friendship and you have mine but that doesn't make us eye to eye as Architects—as no-one knows better than yourself.

Faithfully yours,
Frank Lloyd Wright
Taliesin,
Spring Green,
Wisconsin,
February 3rd, 1931.

[pc ts lmp]

[RETYPED COPY SENT TO LEWIS MUMFORD]
(COPY OF LETTER FROM RAYMOND HOOD TO FRANK LLOYD WRIGHT)

FEBRUARY 16, 1931

Mr. Frank Lloyd Wright,
Taliesin,
Spring Green, Wis.

My dear Frank:

Your letter should have been answered right away, but they have been working me hard days, and keeping me up late nights, besides sending me away on a five day trip since it arrived. This is the first quiet moment I have had.

You can answer as well as I can the question as to whether the Chicago Fair is a private party or not. When a project is started, not by an official party, but by a group of private individuals, whether it is matter of public interest or not, the sponsors must assume the responsibility of appointing the people who are to run it according to their own lights—until at least it is taken over by the public. In this case the original group that got together to promote a fair, elected their Trustees, and Rufus Dawes was made President.

Paul Cret and myself were appointed as the first two architects of the commission by Dawes from a list of architects that has been approved by the Trustees.[1] We two, in turn, nominated the balance of the commission, and our nominations (which were not confined to the original list) were approved by the Trustees. How the original list was made up, and how Cret and myself were selected by Dawes, I do not know, as neither of us had ever met Dawes or the Trustees prior to a telephone invitation to come to Chicago for this purpose. I presume, however, that it was all done by the usual method of discussion, inquiry, and so on.

When we were making up the final nominations, Cret proposed

---

1 Paul Philippe Cret (1876–1945), French architect and educator who emigrated to the United States.

your name among the first. My reaction was that this must be a project directed by a commission of Architects and that you, temperamentally, did not fit on a commission. I felt that you were a strong individualist, and that if an attempt were made to harness you in with other architects, the result would be more apt to be a fight than a fair.

Since then it has always been the intention of the commission to call in other architects to help, and your name has constantly been under consideration. But those of us who want you in on the fair still feel that it must be where you can work independently, without being obliged to correlate your work with the work of some other architect. And in the part of the work that has gone on ahead up to now, such a job has not occurred.

Now I do not consider that in the situation that has developed, there is anything embarrassing,—or to use your own word "insulting," either to you or to the commission. It involves no question of modern art, or of your ability or your accomplishments, for which I, in spite of the fact that I was instrumental in your not being on the commission up to present, have a deep regard and admiration.

I do not claim that I was particularly competent to do the Job that was put up to me, nor do I claim that my judgement has been the best possible under the circumstances. I acted according to my own convictions, and as an architect who is working at the trade, I feel that I have as much right to a conviction about the conduct of an architectural project, as have the critics who appear to be heading up this situation.

I have answered your letter as plainly as I can, but I know that in doing so, there is less chance of forfeiting your friendship than in writing pages of polite ambiguities.

I still admire you very much, even though some of your friends would probably like to crucify me.

As ever,
[signed] Raymond Hood.

P.S. You can use this letter any way you wish. I am obviously speaking only for myself, but it gives you I think the information you want.
[signed] R. M. H.

[pc ts lmp]

[SENT TO LEWIS MUMFORD]

Mr. Raymond Hood,
American Radiator Bldg.,
40 West 30th Street,
New York City.

Dear Ray Hood:

Your plea of guilty puts me, where frankly, I now prefer to belong,—outside.

You were the man I felt I wanted to work with, because I felt I could trust you. The others of course are unknown to me. This hope, false,—I feel I can be more useful to Architecture in our country—definitely as well as politically free from any connection with the Fair.

Stop looking for something to turn up that will leave me out and take me in.

You say the Fair involves no question of modern Art—so I will try to justify your fear and faith in the fight as to expedients the fair would have been were I in it, by a fairer fight—on principle—owing no one anything—no Ray,—not even a grudge, believe me.

And you are not the man to grudge me that fight?

Sincerely yours,
Frank Lloyd Wright,
Taliesin,
Spring Green,
Wisconsin,
February 18, 1931.

P.S. I only regret that you kept this from me so long—and so skillfully.

[pc ts&ms lmp]

4002 LOCUST STREET
LONG ISLAND CITY

29 MARCH 1931

Dear FLW:

Your telegram was totally unexpected: for if ever there was a labor of love my talk that night was such.[1] But I appreciate your generosity & will not make you uncomfortable by questioning it. Enough if I say, very sincerely, many thanks! I daresay there have been repercussions of your reception here; but I have been so deep in work this last month that I haven't heard any. Tell me your news, when you get time. The Museum of Modern Art is going to hold an Architectural Show & Philip Johnson, the young man who is organizing it, would like you to be adequately represented in it.[2] He is a sidekick of H R Hitchcock's, and, among other things, still very young: but I think it would be worth while to give him your attention. He will come West to talk things over with you, I think, if you feel this is necessary. Please consider this an introduction! Sophie joins me in warm greetings to you & Mrs. Wright.

Warmly,
[signed]
Lewis

P.S. Why did no one ever tell me about L. Sullivan's Cedar Rapids Bank[?][3] It seems on paper the best of his later works.

P.P.S. Which tomb of his do you like best[?] You once said; but I don't remember.

[ms flwa]

---

1 Telegram unlocated. Wright evidently wired Mumford an "honorarium" in gratitude for Mumford's testimonial on his behalf on the night of the AUDAC lecture.
2 First mention of *Modern Architecture: International Exhibition*, exhibition, Museum of Modern Art, New York, 10 February 1932 to 23 March 1932, and numerous subsequent American venues; Philip Johnson (b. 1906), American architect, curator, and writer. Johnson and Henry-Russell Hitchcock, Jr. were curators of this exhibition. Museum of Modern Art Director Alfred H. Barr, Jr. coined the term "International Style" around this time to describe the emergent modern architecture in Europe and the United States. On the history of the planning of this exhibition, see Terence Riley, *The International Style: Exhibition 15 and the Museum of Modern Art* (New York: Rizzoli, 1992).
3 Louis H. Sullivan, People's Savings Bank, Cedar Rapids, Iowa, 1909–1911.

Mr. Lewis Mumford,
4112 Gosman Ave.,
Long Island City,
New York.

Dear Lewis:

I know the little money-matter was foolish.[1] But I've had so hard a time the past year getting pennies enough together to keep working—that I've begun to worry about my friends. It has come to me for the first time to wonder how it is all going with them and to view "with anxiety." You would have hurt my feelings by not allowing my intention.

A copy of letter to Johnson. I haven't told you about the European invitations.[2]

Johnson is evidently a feature of the little group Hitchcock is pushing and hangs his hopes on—now emulating the Corbusier. It is not a very talented group, I believe, as far as I know them,—but no doubt helpful if they don't get things too far their way.

They are seeking to start a narrow movement and inasmuch as they have no choice but to all work and think alike,—such is their thinking—, they may succeed with other natural born emulators. This group within group with fixed ideas of the great Idea is always with us. I've seen it in several different forms already,—this is the latest, but by no means the last.

They are all hard-pushing propagandists. And I've observed there is no more conscienceless Propagandist on our Soil than the European—bred when once he grasps the idea that seems to work over here.

The Princeton Lectures are out and here is a first copy to you my friend—.[3]

Some interesting battles are ahead of us.—I look forward with pleasure.

Concerning Sullivan's Cedar Rapids Bank. To show you how difficult is the work of the historian,—and this for your ears alone—the

1 A reference, it would seem, to the "honorarium."

2 Invitations to show the Princeton University exhibition in Holland, Belgium, and Germany.

3 Wright, *Modern Architecture: Being the Kahn Lectures*.

only latter day bank—really Louis Sullivan was the Owatona [*sic*].[4] The others were left more and more to George Elmslie—(my understudy while with Louis Sullivan—) and,—for reasons following,—that means more or less "arcing" back to my own work.[5] This is true particularly of the Cedar Rapids Bank, the Bradley House at Madison, the Babson house at Riverside, Ill[.]—as you may readily see for yourself.[6] George has frail, if any, creative ability,—knew only Sullivan and myself. And his work since leaving the Master was more characteristic of myself than Sullivan. He used to come out to the Oak Park Studio when I was pressed for help and take a hand with me—evenings.[7]

Sullivan knew nothing about residences—as you know. And what George knew—he knew from early work with me—and overtime help.

The Charnley house in Chicago on Center Street I did at home for Adler and Sullivan to help pay my building bills.[8] That house was the forerunner of the Winslow house as you may see if you glance at both together.

So there was,—toward the last,—this "backwash" (as the lieber Meister grew more feeble and discouraged)—by way of George—.[9] When George got out on his own after more than ten years with Sullivan he kept the Sullivanian ornament and added it to my sense of things and my technique in building—as you may see for yourself—by a little study.

I have never regarded the matter as important though at the time I felt it with some resentment. I remember that.

Nearly everything in Life is blended at the edges? <u>No</u> hard and fast lines in Nature you see. The Historian must make them,—and lucky if he gets in the middle of the "blend."

Meiklejohn is out of the University I am sorry to say. And a prospect for such a School as I hoped to establish here at Hillside

---

4 Louis H. Sullivan, National Farmers' Bank, Owatonna, Minnesota, 1906–1908.

5 George Grant Elmslie (1871–1952), American architect.

6 Louis H. Sullivan, Harold C. Bradley Residence, Madison, Wisconsin, 1909; Louis H. Sullivan, Henry Babson Residence (demolished), Riverside, Illinois, 1907.

7 Wright's Residence and Studio, Oak Park, Illinois, 1889–1911.

8 Dankmar Adler (1844–1900), architect, engineer, and partner with Louis H. Sullivan in firm of Adler and Sullivan; Louis H. Sullivan and Frank Lloyd Wright, Charnley Residence, Chicago, 1891.

9 Frank Lloyd Wright's German term of endearment for Louis H. Sullivan.

looms in Chicago as "the Allied Arts and Industries." It is severing a hasty connection with the Art-Institute to go along with me—I have reason to believe. In which case you will have a hand in it.[10]

Strange. I had to wait 27 years for some one in my own country to ask to publish my work—. And what better could I ask, finally, than to have Princeton make the offer?

The cover is gay—reproducing one of the "abstractions for children"—from the exhibit? The "Sahuaro."[11]

Affectionately,
[signed]
F.Ll.W.
Frank Lloyd Wright,
Taliesin,
Spring Green,
Wisconsin,
April 7, 1931.

[pc ts&ms lmp]

10 Art Institute of Chicago.
11 Frank Lloyd Wright, design for cover of *Liberty Magazine*, November 1926.

[SENT TO LEWIS MUMFORD]

Mr. Philip Johnson,
424 E. 52nd Str.,
New York City.

My dear Philip Johnson:

You probably do not know that an exhibition of my work including all available plans and drawings, 450 photographs and five models is just under way to Europe. Six European Governments have invited the exhibition and undertaken all expense of transport and showing in the principal cities of Europe—at various national academies or museums as the case may be.

This leaves me flat for material for any other exhibit—until next September. The exhibition will return about that time. We have designed the whole as a complete unit.

But come up anyway;—there may be something I can do and I should like to meet whether or no—.

Sincerely yours,
Frank Lloyd Wright
Taliesin,
Spring Green,
Wisconsin,
April 3rd, 1931.

[cc ts flwa]

Mr. Lewis Mumford,
4112 Gosman Ave.,
Long Island City,
New York.

Dear Lewis:

Concerning preface to "the book" I wrote Smith as inclosed [*sic*].[1] And am suggesting the Princeton University Press ask you to review the book for the *New York Times*. But maybe that request must come from the "Times"? I don't know.—

Anyhow you would do it more fairly than anyone else—for not so many know what it is all about anyway—.

Sincerely yours,
Frank Lloyd Wright,
Taliesin,
April 8, 1931.

[cc ts flwa]

---

1 E. Baldwin Smith (1888–1956), American architectural historian, writer, and educator; Smith wrote the preface to Wright, *Modern Architecture*.

4002 LOCUST STREET
LONG ISLAND CITY, N.Y.

27 APRIL 1931

Dear F L W:

I am finishing up my book—45,000 words in two weeks!—and have scarcely breath left to thank you for your rich and handsome book, so packed with good things.[1] Geddes has the measles and my book must be finished: so be patient!

More later.

Warmly,
[signed]
Lewis

[ms flwa]

---

1 Mumford, *The Brown Decades*; Wright, *Modern Architecture*.

Mr. Lewis Mumford,
4002 Locust Street,
Long Island City,
New York.

Dear Lewis:

The *New York Evening Post* asked me for a criticism of Radio City.[1] I sent them this. When you've read it send it back with your comment.

Sincerely,
Frank Lloyd Wright,
Taliesin,
Spring Green,
Wisconsin,
June 20, 1931.

[cc ts flwa]

1 Frank Lloyd Wright, "Architect Calls Radio City False: Frank Lloyd Wright Declares Plan Exaggerates Worst Elements: Sees Rentals Only Theme," *New York Evening Post* (30 June 1931): 4; reprinted as "Radio City" in *Frank Lloyd Wright: Collected Writings, Volume 3, 1931–1939*, edited by Bruce Brooks Pfeiffer with an introduction by Kenneth Frampton (New York: Rizzoli in association with the Frank Lloyd Wright Foundation, 1993), 59–62. Radio City was an early name for the entire Rockefeller Center complex.

AMENIA, N.Y.

27 JUNE 1931

Dear F. L. W.:

We are here till October—all of us having a high old time, splashing color over the interior of this ramshackle & almost ancient farmhouse, grubbing in the garden, and hacking away the plaster & lath that sometimes conceals handsome bricks or almost adequate beams! Meanwhile, I have finished *The Brown Decades* & have, I think, brought to light all sorts of buried treasures, most of which you are doubtless familiar with. Your book has delighted everyone I've shown it to: it is a landmark.[1] It will whet people's appetite for the biography.[2] I can say nothing about your article on Radio City except Amen. (Did you happen to see my Amen in last week's *New Yorker*?)[3] The mail that brought your essay brought me letters of congratulation from a. a N.Y. mortgage specialist, and b. from Dr. Ralph Adams Cram: so it looks as though, except for the honorable R. H. and H. W. C., the votes against Radio City were unanimous.[4] Should the *Evening Post* be idiots enough to turn your article down, please send it to the *New Republic*. The bottom is dropping out of the skyscraper business: there is nothing to keep up the inflation. It will be a fine time for those of us who have kept close to the ground.

Sophie joins me in warm good wishes to you both.

Affectionately,
[signed]
Lewis

[ms flwa]

1 Wright, *Modern Architecture*.

2 Wright, *An Autobiography*.

3 Lewis Mumford, "Frozen Music or Solidified Static? Reflections on Radio City," *New Yorker* 7 (20 June 1931): 28–36.

4 Ralph Adams Cram (1863–1942), American architectural historian and writer; Raymond Hood; Harvey W. Corbett.

AMENIA, NEW YORK

14 AUGUST 1931

Dear F.L.W. :

It was fun to see Behrendt's account of the exhibition: so acute on the whole, and so appreciative and honest.[1] Behrendt is a friend of mine: it is through him that *Sticks and Stones* was published in Germany: so I warmed to the article all the more.[2] Catherine Bauer has told me how nice you have been to her: she is a close friend, too, and we have had more than one long talk together in which you were not only the principal object of discussion, but served as battledore and shuttlecock between our respective philosophies of architecture and life: I have had something of an influence on her, but it was nothing in comparison with the immediate and overwhelming effect of your own book: and I daresay she has had some influence on me, too.[3] She is a brilliant and fearless and honest girl, and has the best natural gifts in critical thinking of anyone I know now under thirty: so she is worth, as perhaps you discovered from her review, whatever pains and attention you have the opportunity to bestow on her. Douglas has real gifts, too, of course, but Catherine is less erratic, I think; she has a certain tenacity and comprehensiveness . . .[4] My book on the *Brown Decades* is all but ready to go on the press, and you shall of course have a copy at an early date. I hope other people do not find it quite as tedious as I do; but unfortunately, I was compelled to write the book in sections, and so I missed the exhilaration of diving in at one end of the pool and coming up, without taking an extra breath, at the other. At all events, in the architecture section, it corrects and rectifies a lot of things that were missing in *Sticks and Stones*. Having finished the *Brown Decades*, I am back again on the book I started last summer, when I was so miser-

---

1 Walter Curt Behrendt, "Frank Lloyd Wright: Zur Ausstellung in der Akademie der Künste in Berlin," *Frankfurter Zeitung und Handelsblatt* (30 June 1931).
2 Lewis Mumford, *Vom Blockhaus zum Wolkenkratzer: Eine Studie über Amerikanische Architektur und Zivilisation*, translated by M. Mauthner (Berlin: Bruno Cassirer Verlag, [1925]).
3 Catherine Bauer (1905–1964), American writer, educator, and housing reformer with whom Mumford was romantically involved between 1929–1932.
4 Douglas Haskell.

ably ill: the original draft is so bad, that it is practically a new job, and I find it amusing.[5] Heaven knows when it will be finished. Sophie and I and little Geddes alternate between cultivating the garden and scraping and hacking at and painting this ramshackle house: we have much to occupy us, and get plenty of fun out of it, which is fortunate, since the infantile paralysis epidemic deprives us of visitors from New York, and its shadow might even spoil a pleasant hour if we looked up too often from our work. I trust life treats you kindly this summer. Please remember both of us to your wife and believe me,

Affectionately
[signed]
Lewis

[ts flwa]

5 Lewis Mumford, "Form and Personality/Form and Civilization," unpublished typescript.

Mr. Lewis Mumford,
New York City.

Dear Lewis:

This may interest you—: I would like to know if it "gets over" in the German or is distorted.[1]

I thought it time to go to the mat. The thing is all over Europe by now.

Behrend [*sic*] picked me up at once contra Corbusier.

I've sent a copy to Catherine Bauer.

I replied to her very characteristic note and hope she doesn't mind teasing—for I called her "Communist Catherine." There are lots of names she could call me to even up.

The three evenings at the New School are Sept. 16, 17, and 18th and the 19th, we sail for Rio to make the award of the Columbus Memorial returning Oct. 26th.[2]

A job on my hands.

I can't vote for anything the previous trio recommended. I guess I am going down to register a minority report.

N.B. I have a job. New home in Washington, D. C.[3]

Your friend,

Taliesin,
Spring Green,
Sept. 10, 1931.

[cc ts flwa]

---

1 Frank Lloyd Wright, "Die Mechanisierung und die Materialien," *Die Form* 6 (September 1931): 341–349.

2 Frank Lloyd Wright, Lectures at the New School for Social Research, New York (16, 17, and 18 September 1931). Along with two other architects, Wright was invited in October 1931 to Rio de Janeiro, Brazil to judge the competition for the Christopher Columbus Memorial Lighthouse.

3 Project for Mildred E. Curran Residence, Washington, D.C., 1931.

AMENIA, NEW YORK

15 SEPTEMBER 1931

Dear F.L.W.:

I first heard of your coming last week, when Johnson invited me to sit in the discussion.[1] Alas! that I can't: on Thursday I have to go up to Dartmouth to open a course on city planning, and I won't be back until the twenty-second.[2] If only we could have had a glimpse of you and your wife up here. We both look forward to seeing you in New York when you return. They did an excellent job in translating you: far better than usually happens in my experience; and Behrendt's discussion seemed to me very intelligent: he makes again the point I made in my review of Hitchcock's monograph—that Le Corbusier is obsessed with geometry and classicism, and imputes to the machine qualities that do not exist there, and so would put modern architecture in what is essentially a static formula. I am naturally on your side with respect to everything except "individuality"—which I trust won't make it seem to you that I am not on your side at all. I still cannot conceive of a city in which each separate work of architecture would be conceived in complete freedom: if this sometimes seems to happen in medieval cities it is only because the conventions were so universal and so rigidly obeyed. But we must argue this out at some other time, when you are not preparing to take ship—if by the time you get this Catherine has not put the same matter with her own special emphasis. I am keeping the Frankfort paper, at least until you come back.[3] With warm greetings from both Sophie and myself—

Affectionately
[signed]
Lewis

[ts flwa]

---

1 Alvin Johnson (1874–1971), American educator and director of New School for Social Research.

2 Dartmouth College in Hanover, New Hampshire, where Mumford was visiting professor of art between 1929–1935.

3 Behrendt, "Frank Lloyd Wright: Zur Ausstellung in der Akademie der Künste in Berlin."

Mr. Lewis Mumford,
4002 Locust Street,
Long Island City,
N.Y.

My dear Lewis:

I've read "The Brown Decades" you so kindly sent me and it is a useful work in your splendid style. I didn't agree in toto but admire and respect.

I was sorry to see so little of you in New York—intending to see you if I saw no one else. And the stupidity of wandering around in the Lehigh Starret building while you were waiting for me at 41 west 12th street rises to plague me still.

Dutchy and I saw something of Catherine Bauer in New York.[1]

The Guggenheim has asked me for a recommendation for the new work she wants to do and I gave my best—but wrote her what I thought of her thesis.[2] You know what I must think about that. Enclosed is a copy of what I think about it for your files if you care for it.

I imagine I have disillusioned Catherine and am sorry. She has a good mind but, like Hitchcock is "international-minded" as a complete formula instead of only so far as such standardization doesn't take the life of individuality.

Also herewith a copy of the roar at the *Vanity Fair* insinuations (December number).[3]

I read your *New Yorker* criticism of the Metropolitan.[4] Without seeing the show I know you are right and how effective! I hope you don't go off the *New Yorker*.[5] And Lewis, please don't ever fall out with me. I should be afraid of you—.

Dutchy has gone home—. He is too much of a lyrical egoist to be ideal for the school but he has enough good qualities to make it worthwhile to try. He makes my egocentricity look like a single color in the

---

1 Wright's nickname for H. Th. Wijdeveld.

2 John Simon Guggenheim Foundation, New York.

3 John Cushman Fistere, "Poets in Steel," *Vanity Fair* 37 (December 1931): 58–59, 98.

4 Lewis Mumford, "Contemporary Industrial Art," *New Yorker* 7 (14 November 1931): 36–42.

5 Mumford joined the staff of *The New Yorker* in fall 1931 as architecture critic in charge of "The Sky Line" column.

spectrum while he has them all. This surprised me. I thought I was the limit.

I think of you and Mrs. Mumford with affection—wishing I had you closer. It is trying—this standing alone—but what recompense beside the affection he gives and receives from his own hearth,—beside the joy he takes out of and puts in to his work has any man?

Sounds "virtuous"?

I have hopes of Wisconsin for you and for Catherine too, this winter. I see Glen Frank to put the case next week.[6]

I decided to enclose, too, the prospectus of the school, worked out while Dutchy was here.[7] Tell me what you think about it in a few lines. I am realizing what it means for a writer to write personal letters to any but his own, and they get few.

He doesn't have time or much inclination.

Affectionately,
[signed]
F.Ll.W.
Frank Lloyd Wright
Taliesin Spring Green
Wisconsin Telephone 110
December 9th. 1931.

[pc ts&ms lmp]

6 Glen Frank (1887–1940), American educator and president of the University of Wisconsin.
7 Frank Lloyd Wright, "The Hillside Home School of the Allied Arts," privately printed, 1931; reprinted in *Frank Lloyd Wright: Collected Writings, Volume 3, 1931–1939*, 39–49.

1932

As the February opening of the Museum of Modern Art's *Modern Architecture: International Exhibition* approaches, Wright threatens to withdraw his work due to differences with the curators. Mumford intervenes and convinces Wright to reconsider. The exhibition, which begets the term "International Style," opens as planned with Wright's House on the Mesa project prominently featured. The architect soon turns his attention to the publication of his autobiography and the launching of his school, known as the Taliesin Fellowship.

4002 LOCUST STREET
LONG ISLAND CITY, N.Y.

10 JANUARY 1932

Dear F.L.W.:

Your letter is a month old already, and I am a month older too: the gray hairs in my head have increased, the furrows in my brow deepened, the vertebrae in my back have sunk together with far more than a month's worth of damage, as a result of a perfectly maddening bout of lectures and articles I have been doing: this and this alone accounts for my long silence and my failure to wish you in good season a happy and triumphantly laborious New Year! I have still a couple of weeks to go before I return to quiet waters: but in the meanwhile, I must at least say hello, and thank you for the valuable budget of papers you sent me along with your letter. They are very helpful to that part of me who has assigned himself to be historian of American culture; and quite apart from that, I have enjoyed them and profited by them. I knew you wouldn't altogether like *The Brown Decades*: the truth is I don't altogether like it either: although we probably are dissatisfied by different parts of it! But we have so many things in common, including our sense of the meaningfulness of life itself, that our differences, however real, don't keep us very far apart: perhaps they all go back to the fact that I am a product of the city, who has learned to like and to live in the country; whereas you are a product of the country who has never really found much for himself in the city! But that is too simple: and the differences remain so unimportant that I see no reason for diminishing them or trying to reconcile them. Your criticism of Catherine Bauer's thesis is worth publishing by itself: but she was far from disillusioned by it. She is the most promising person around these parts: a real mind, a fine courageous spirit, large possibilities of growth—although, as with every girl, the chances of being diverted and deflected are greater with her than they would be, I think, if she were a young man. The learned Hitchcock visited me the other day: he has almost become a disciple of yours, much though you might prefer to see him remain on the hostile side of the fence. His real deficiency is that he deals with reality best through the medium of paper: photographs and documents show him at his best: real sights and experiences leave him cold. The weakness of the second hand. My own direct approach puzzles him a little, I think: but maybe I flatter myself.

If only you were nearer! Sophy has been flourishing this winter, serving her apprenticeship as teacher in one of the best of the experimental schools here, the City and Country, where young Geddes also goes: it would be such fun if only our families could have something of each other. . . . I have heard nothing from Wisconsin, and have not been able to extract a letter from John Gaus: but I suppose he is busy helping to run the state of Wisconsin. . . . [1] Fritz writes to Catherine: but I haven't heard a word from him, either.[2] I expect to spend the late winter in New York, recuperating from the last three months; but I am down for a lecture in Chicago the first week in March, and if I can possibly manage it, I shall go to Europe early in May. If they have cooked up a revolution or a war or a French occupation of Germany by then—all of these seem likely—I'll content myself with England, Holland, and Scandinavia; but if the world as a whole is in flames, which seems to me also quite likely, I shall retire to my Dutchess County acre and put in my vegetables early.[3] In the meanwhile, somewhere, somewhen, I trust we will meet: all blessings to you.

Affectionately,
[signed]
Lewis

[ts flwa]

1 John M. Gaus (1894–1969), American political scientist.

2 Frederick A. Gutheim (1908–1993), American architectural historian and writer.

3 Dutchess County, New York, where the Mumfords' farmhouse was located.

Mr. Lewis Mumford,
4002 Locust Street,
Long Island City, N.Y.

Dear Lewis:

I have walked into another propaganda-trap, tho [*sic*] a trap not consciously so designed, and have pulled out at the risk of seeming ignoble and ungenerous.

The enclosed letter will explain.

I consented to join the affair thinking I would be among my peers: I heard only of Corbusier, Mies et al.[1] I found a handpicked select group including Hood and Neutra.[2]

One drives the flu-flu bird off the nest only to find the cuckoo there, it seems? Well, no great matter. No, but I want to explain things to you, so you will not be ignorant of the reason for my stand.

As for exception to Neutra. It applies to a type I have learned to dislike, by cumulative experience, and to suffer from.

He came here to work, 1924 I think, after a sojourn with Holabird and Root, marking-in plumbing on plans.[3] He was worthless here @$30.00 per week and a living for his family, wife, child, mother in law, and left after nine months. Previous to this he had been in the publicity department of the city of Vienna, had gone from there to Mendelsohn, and they built several cottages together since published by Neutra with Mendelsohn's name deleted. Characteristic!

He went to Los Angeles to join Schindler.[4] I think both are jews [*sic*] and were friends in Vienna. He wrote a book as one familiar with building methods in America, "Wie Baut Amerika."[5] Pretentious in the circumstances! There his publicity training began to work. He got a half-baked building he called the "health house," built on Corbusier-lines absolutely, of which I learned in an interesting manner.[6] Making

---

1 Ludwig Mies van der Rohe (1886–1969), German architect who subsequently immigrated to the United States.

2 Richard Neutra (1892–1970), Austrian architect who immigrated to the United States and who worked for Wright in 1924.

3 Holabird and Root, American architectural firm based in Chicago.

4 Rudolph Michael Schindler (1887–1953), Viennese architect who immigrated to the United States and who worked for Wright between 1918–1921.

5 Richard Neutra, *Wie Baut Amerika* (Stuttgart: J. Hoffmann, 1927).

some plans for a Miss Noble, whose mother was the owner of some flat-buildings in Los Angeles, the mother brought a reprinted sheet of press-notices about this marvelous house, "the details of which had been under consideration in the Neutra brain for four years."[7] It had taken several years just to make the details of the iron work etc. (stock-sash). The collection of, evidently inspired, notices had been made up with a photo of Neutra in the middle, re-photographed and re-printed—propagandizing this "great" European architect as the Messiah of the new system—hailing the order of a new day. The contractor, waiting at the door, said he was interested with Neutra and had been sent by him,—and Neutra would produce plans for Mrs. Noble to look at, at no charge at all to her, if she would allow him to do so?

This was about three years after he had left Taliesin.

Two years ago I received a notice from Schindler's ex-wife, Sophie, who was now acting as press agent for the pair, to the effect that they wanted to star Frank Lloyd Wright in Los Angeles and had arranged an exhibit, having gone to the expense of having photographs made of my work, (the way they liked to see it), and would put themselves on either side.[8] I thought very little of the matter until they opened a show under the ballyhoo "Exhibition of work of Three Architects of International renown."[9] The show was thus to tour America! The game was visible, and I wired to take me out. They did not take me out until the show was all over in Los Angeles, but did refrain from taking me "on tour." I have never seen the photographs they used.

Then came the International architectural school in Los Angeles—Neutra and Schindler—with false pretenses in every line of the ballyhoo. Neutra = "Lecturer at the School of Social Research" as though a regular![10] He spoke once to a small audience. & "Associate of Erich Mendelsohn" was another, convenient now. Neutra taking the circuit, (at mother in law's expense, I suppose) and lecturing as "great-archi-

---

6 Lovell Residence (Health House), Los Angeles, 1927–1929.

7 Elizabeth Noble, client of Frank Lloyd Wright.

8 Sophie Pauline Gibling Schindler (1893–1977), writer and wife of Rudolph Michael Schindler.

9 *Contemporary Creative Architecture of California*, exhibition, 27–29 April 1930, Exhibition Gallery Education Building, University of California at Los Angeles, and subsequent venues in Los Angeles and in several western states and Hawaii.

10 New School for Social Research, New York.

tect-in-America"—when he went to Europe, and "great-architect-in-Europe" when in America, and "great-architect-in-both-countries" when in Japan, where he went to follow up a friendship with a Japanese couple, who were here at the same time he was.[11]

Well, out of the flimsiest qualifications imaginable, he seems to have ballyhooed himself to the point where I now find him. Hitchcock & Johnson supporting him because, I imagine, he was the Internationalist—propaganda over here and a "ringer" for the adored Corbusier?

Perhaps we should admire this—and well, you will say, what of it? And I would say so, too, but for the fact that this imitation of our national high-power salesmanship is what is the matter with everything in our blessed, damned country.

And any modesty, or probity, or prowess any man might have or pursue is wasted, or rendered futile, by the brazen pretense of any man with little or no talent, so he takes the proper attitudes and can make the proper noises with his mouth. I am against making star-architects by such methods but I will be in the hopeless minority.

Neutra is the eclectic "up to date," copying the living.

Hood was the eclectic copying the dead,—is now the improved eclectic copying the living. I do not propose to "take the road" in fellowship with eclecticism in any form! It is too late to compromise now.

I will stand aside, as I've said, and let the ballyhoo go by. I think, however, I should not meantime be silent or give in.

So I shall arrange a show—contra—in New York to follow this "foreign" one. It will now be foreign almost entirely, Hood excepted, for Lescaze is here by late adoption.[12] I doubt if Neutra is yet a citizen! Not that that matters particularly—except, before the cuckoo (the International) has hatched the eggs, it has laid in the nest of modern architecture,—the song of the modern should be clearly heard in no equivocal circumstances!

When you come in January, you must come to us at Taliesin, or I shall be disappointed to the breaking point. Let me know when!

I, too, wish our families were nearer to each other. We have not

---

11 Kameki Tsuchiura (1897–1996) and Nobu Tsuchiura (1900–1998), Japanese draftsmen employed by Frank Lloyd Wright in early 1920s.

12 William Lescaze (1896–1969), Swiss architect who emigrated to the United States.

much companionship. And what is the matter at U. of W. is money. They have cut everything down to the quick and are now unable to pay. I got Wijdeveld a lecture @ $50.—finally. A lyrical song about how he and Berlage started the modern movement in Europe, Gropius soon alongside—, (the thing has as many pedigrees now floating from banners on the band-wagon, as there are peddlers)—until he broke in a paean of praise for "the ship in the storm"—meaning me.[13]

He is a songful speaker and they liked it—most of them.

My love to you, dear man—.

Enclosed with letter to P.J. a short article "to the Neuter" inspired by a well written "writing off" of Architecture by an "I Believe" in the ["]T-Square" of the T-Square Club.[14]

By the way, in this same magazine is an article of the type in question by Neutra—the cottages he describes are three built with Mendelsohn.[15] Widjeveld [*sic*] says he asked N. to speak in Amsterdam and he wore out the audience with 76 slides, 65 of them of his "health house."

Douglas Haskell describes him as "pretty thin" after knowing him in N.Y.—but Hitchcock likes the "thin" I guess.

Faithfully—and affectionately,
[signed]
F.Ll.W
• Frank Lloyd Wright
Taliesin • Spring-Green
Wisconsin telephone 110
January 19th. 1932.

I want you to tell me directly, no matter how uncomplimentary, what you think of my action? Will you?

[signed]
FLlW

[pc ts&ms lmp]

---

13 Hendrik Petrus Berlage (1856–1934), Dutch architect.

14 Philip Johnson; Frank Lloyd Wright, "To the Neuter," unpublished essay, 1932, Norman N. Rice, "I Believe . . . ," T Square 2 (January 1932): 24–25, 34–35. "Neuter" is Wright's derisive term for the "International Style," but it may also be a pun on Richard Neutra's surname.

15 Richard J. Neutra, "New Architecture Has a Pedigree," *T-Square* 2 (January 1932): 9–10, 40.

[RETYPED LETTER SENT TO LEWIS MUMFORD]

(COPY.)

Mr. Philip Johnson,
1007 Chatham Phoenix Building,
Long Island City, N.Y.

My dear Philip:

There is not much use in writing this letter. It will convince you of nothing except that I am hard to deal with and an uncompromising egotist as per propaganda and schedule.

All right. So be it. I shall at least have the luxury of living up to that part, such as it is, for which I am cast. I am going to step aside and let the procession go by with its band-wagon. I find I don't speak the same language nor am I in step with its aims and purposes. Architecture to me is something else.

If you had made the character of the show a little clearer to me in the beginning, we might have saved some waste motion and expense, but I hope there is not much of that by now[,] money is so hard to find.

My telegram explains most of what I have to say.[1]

I find myself rather a man without a country, architecturally speaking, at the present time. If I keep on working another five years, I shall be at home again, I feel sure.

But meantime the scramble of the propagandist "international" for the band-wagon must have taken place and the procession must be well on its way, without me.

It seems to me, I see too much at stake for me to countenance a hand-picked group of men in various stages of eclecticism by riding around the country with them, as though I approved of them and their work as modern, when I distinctly do not only disapprove but positively condemn them.

I respect Corbusier, admire van der Rohe, like Haesler and many good men not in your show, if the list is as indicative as intended.[2]

---

1 Telegram from Frank Lloyd Wright to Philip Johnson, 18 January 1932, archives, Museum of Modern Art, New York.

2 Otto Haesler (1880–1962), German architect and planner.

Howe is respectable and Lescaze, so far as I know, though a fledgling.[3]

I could feel at home in a show including them, and such younger men as were earnestly at work trying to build noble and beautiful buildings, as I did when I was younger, and willing to patiently establish themselves as architects by that honest route—and claim success, step by step, as earned.

But I am sick and tired of the pretense of men who will elect a style, old or new, and get a building badly built by the help of some contractor and then publicize it as a notable achievement. This hits not one man only, but a type of which you have chosen a willing and busy exponent in Neutra. You know my opinion of Hood and his tribe?

Propaganda is a vice in our country. High power salesmanship is a curse. I can at least mind my own business, if I can get any to mind, and not compete or consort with what are to me disreputable examples of disreputable methods that will get our future architecture nothing but an "international style." A cut paper style at that. I am aware of your sympathies in that direction and of Russell's—and was prepared to respect both of you in it until I see the taint of propaganda in the personal examples you prefer.

I believe both of you sincere, but you are both beginning, and probably unaware of much that is too thin to wash and too false in color not to fade.

But that is no reason why I should join your procession and belie my own principles both of architecture and conduct?

I am aware, too, of the ammunition this act of mine furnishes my enemies. Oh yes, I have so many! No man more.

But my eye is on a goal better worth trying for, even if I am called in before I reach it. If I am, I shall at least not have sold out!

Believe me, Philip, I am sorry. Give my best to Russell Hitchcock and I expect to see you both here at Taliesin early next summer—with your wives. If you haven't got them now you will have them by then?

Sincerely yours,
(signed) Frank Lloyd Wright.
January 19th. 1932.

[pc ts lmp]

---

3 George Howe (1886–1955), American architect and partner with William Lescaze in the firm of Howe and Lescaze.

[SENT TO LEWIS MUMFORD]

TO THE NEUTER.

The eunuch has certain advantages by way of his operation. The urge of his pro-creative power, let's say, if his character is good, gives way to a calm attitude of intellectual appreciation. Himself now vicarious, if at all, it is the "formula" that intrigues him, or else, desire still alive, he is maddened and envious. In a sad case. Sterilized to the point of "intellectuality" as substitute for creative power, in any case, his resources are those of apperception instead of feeling.

So it is not surprising at this juncture that the "internationalist" should so soon go off virility of spirit and try to substitute, for feeling in action, a vicarious mental formula as habit.

Not surprising because this equivalent of the consequences of the operation—impotence, on his part, is the result of over-indulgence = sentimentality, or the practice of self-abuse = eclecticism.

But, Nature (the creative mind) her custom holds, let shame (the "style internationale") say what it will.

The human spirit still has a soul that will not be made impotent. Nor consciously nor subconsciously will she make a neuter. She will make the man of her choice claim his human birthright, however the abuse may go. Let's shamelessly call the birthright "individuality," for one thing, and be suspect by all those whose attributes of character have never risen above personal idiosyncrasy and that means, among others, the Neuters.

We have prohibition because a few fools can't carry their liquor. We have the internationalist formula for art because we have sentimentality and eclecticism improved as a formula.

The vicarious attitude turns the matter over to Society's intellectual appreciation. To take the abuse of the thing for the real thing, condemn the reality and exalt the formula. This, it is, to be a neuter.

What we call art and architecture are true love-affairs. It has not yet been given by nature that all men should function above the belt to the same degree. And this quality of love in men or the capacity for it, perhaps, has been growing small while the capacity for lust is much the same in all men as in animals. It is over this blind instinct of lust the eunuch has the advantage of being unable to act.

And I believe that, speaking to the profane figure we started with, it is a too long continued rendezvous with lust that has made the manhood of our century the eunuch as neuter.

Though rendered impotent the neuter is not a total loss. He has his uses, as has the eunuch, as mentor. But do not let him imagine Love is dead because he has ceased to function. The Twentieth Century, notwithstanding the prostitution of the Nineteenth, still has men with capacity for love, who will create anew and fructify the future refusing vicarious trading whatever, in and upon the immediate present, as any formula.

It would be surprising if this probability were recognized by the neuter and placed among his intellectual appreciations—because he would not then be neuter. Though vicarious, he would still be on the side of life for others at least.

But to a neuter all men are neuters. His impotence accords only envy to the potent. The impulse of neutrality (or impotence) when it comes to this true love-affair that is creative art is naturally willing to transfer the creative function to society as a mental matter, and say, "it is better so." But only quieter so for them—as far as they go, I should say. And since the neuter now is the grand majority this may be right enough to temporarily serve the purposes of the age we are about to try to live in.

Such human nature as excess of success with the prostitute (the Nineteenth Century) has left to us, may be content for a time, the rendezvous with the prostitute having incapacitated the majority for the love that is art and architecture. But nature is recuperative beyond anticipation or belief. She will have her way with the neuter by way of the potent individual and not the neuter his way with her.

Learning him, so soon as he attempts her with his formula, she will cast him forth, sans culotte.

Do you think he will then be really more useful to society with his "operation" than the man of feeling who, falling in love with nature, succeeds with her?

Frank Lloyd Wright,
Taliesin,
Spring Green,
Wisconsin,
January 13th. 1932.

[pc cc ts&ms lmp]

[TELEGRAM]

Received at SPRING GREEN, WIS
AU M 80 DL
UD NEWYORK NY 1108 AM JAN 21 1932

FRANK LLOYD WRIGHT,
TALIESIN, SPRINGGREEN WIS.

YOUR ABSENCE FROM MODERN MUSEUMS ARCHITECTURE SHOW WOULD BE CALAMITY[.] PLEASE RECONSIDER YOUR REFUSAL[.] I HAVE NO CONCERN WHATEVER ON BEHALF OF MUSEUM BUT AM INTERESTED IN YOUR OWN PLACE AND INFLUENCE STOP WE NEED YOU AND CANNOT DO WITHOUT YOU STOP YOUR WITHDRAWAL WILL BE USED BY THAT LOW RASCAL HOOD TO HIS OWN GLORY AND ADVANTAGE STOP AS FOR COMPANY THERE IS NO MORE HONORABLE POSITION THAN TO BE CRUCIFIED BETWEEN TWO THIEVES[.] PLEASE WIRE YOUR OKAY[.]

AFFECTIONATELY[,]
LEWIS. 1042 AM

[flwa]

[TELEGRAM]

Received at 4004–58 STREET WOODSIDE N.Y.
NBQ33 33 DL=SPRINGGREEN WIS JAN 21 212P

LEWIS MUMFORD=
4002 LOCUST AVE LONGISLANDCITY NY =

ALL RIGHT LEWIS YOUR SINCERE FRIENDSHIP TRUSTED I WILL STAY IN THE NEWYORK SHOW[.] THE TWO EXCEPTIONS I MADE WERE CHIEFLY IMPORTANT BECAUSE SHOWING UP THE SHOW AS THE USUAL POLITICS AND PROPAGANDA=

FRANK LLOYD WRIGHT
412P.

[pc lmp]

4002 LOCUST STREET
LONG ISLAND CITY

23 JANUARY 1932

Dear F.L.W.:

I don't know which gave me more pleasure: your letter with its enclosures, or the telegram which was lying on top when I got home that night. Your letter because of all the good things it said, and because of the new triumph, the house on the Mesa, an altogether brilliant and satisfying piece of work, which greeted me in it: or your telegram because it assured me that this and other things would have an opportunity to influence people who might otherwise think that the barren and imitative as well as dishonest Hood was an exponent of modern architecture.[1] The withdrawal would have been a real blow to architecture: for the show is scheduled to spend three years on the road, touring the country, and Hood's publicity gang would have made it appear that he was the only American architect worthy of being represented: they would probably have gone the length of hinting, as that rascal did in the *Vanity Fair* article, that you had nothing to show. Johnson is a queer fish: unfortunately, he is the only person around with the time or the money to get together any sort of show; and I never expected at the beginning, when I commended him to you, that one would be able to approve of the entire exhibition: it was enough, from my point of view, that he was eager to give a full representation of you. Unless I mistake Hitchcock's casual conversation, he is much nearer to you than you imagine: certainly far nearer than when he was doing that Cahier d'art introduction—though, hell! that's not saying very much, is it?[2] I have written the introduction to the Housing Section of the show: but have scrupulously kept out of suggesting items even for that tiny piece of it: the whole thing represents Johnson and Hitchcock.[3] No matter what its errors of omission and commission, I think the show will be worth while having and worth

1 Project for a House on the Mesa, Denver, Colorado, 1931.

2 Henry-Russell Hitchcock, Jr., *Frank Lloyd Wright* (Paris: Cahiers d'Art, [1928]).

3 Lewis Mumford, "Housing" in *Modern Architecture: International Exhibition* (New York: Museum of Modern Art, 1932), 179–192.

while being in; and I am grateful for your confidence in my judgement. I am not due in Chicago until 2 March: so perhaps you'll be in the East before I reach the West. Sophie and I both hope to see you soon again.

Hastily
[signed]
Lewis

[ts flwa]

Mr. Lewis Mumford,
4002 Locust Street,
Long Island City, N.Y.

Dear Lewis:

I have conceded capitulation to the New York show not because I believe it more than internationalist propaganda but because I took your judgement as to the reaction of withdrawal. I now believe you are right.

I feel I have been used merely to give authority to the exploitation but, even so, no great harm if I come back quickly. I feel, with such strength as I now have in models and drawings, I should have a show of my own starting in New York and going elsewhere as seems desirable.[1]

Will you look into this far enough to suggest the best place for this? The European show is on its way back and we will soon have seven beautiful models and a fine collection of original drawings. The new theatre [is] one of them.[2] A show, I imagine, richer and more significant than the internationalist propaganda.

The expense will be transportation only and small,—$125.00 will cover it probably—outside our own effort.

Have you influence at the Museum of Modern Art? Would you see Mrs. Harry Payne Whitney for me?[3] She is most friendly.

Would you be interested to lead the Taliesin Fellowship with Mrs. Mumford according to prospectus enclosed?[4]

---

1 Wright is evidently proposing another New York showing of the exhibition that had originated at Princeton and subsequently been on view at the Architectural League of New York before traveling to venues in Europe.

2 Project for a New Theater, Woodstock, New York, 1931.

3 Gertrude Vanderbilt Whitney (1875–1942), sculptor and art patron; Wright has evidently mistaken the Museum of Modern Art for the Whitney Museum of American Art, which Whitney founded in 1930.

4 Frank Lloyd Wright, "The Taliesin Fellowship," privately printed, 1932; reprinted in *Frank Lloyd Wright: Collected Writings, Volume 3, 1931–1939*, 157–166. The Taliesin Fellowship, initiated on 15 October 1932, superceded Wright's plan for the Hillside Home School for the Allied Arts. The Fellowship was based at Taliesin, Wright's residence and studio in Spring Green, Wisconsin. In 1937 construction began on Taliesin West, a winter residence and studio for Wright and the Fellowship in Scottsdale, Arizona. Thereafter, the Wrights and the members of the Fellowship spent their summers at Taliesin and their winters at Taliesin West.

We have at this time approximately 25–35 applications from young men who would like to come. And this on the strength of the rumor abroad that such a school would open!

Faithfully

February 1st. 1932.

[cc ts flwa]

Mr. Lewis Mumford,
4002 Locust Street,
Long Island City, N.Y.

My dear Lewis:

I thought I would better send you the proposed contract between Wijdeveld and myself to scan and also his former and recent reactions to the proposition.

To tell the truth if I could keep the fellowship primarily our own on our own ground I would like it better. I am growing suspicious of "internationalism." (Enclosed a letter to thank Norman Rice for a little more light on that subject.)[1] Can't we manage a group of our own somehow?

If Wijdeveld wants to come we can take him as one of the associates as architect and his wife as musician.[2] She is talented I believe. But it is a great responsibility for me to allow him to come with his whole family to a strange country (three grown up children), closing up a career over there, which—if I can believe him—has been in many respects very successful.

Affectionately,
[signed]
F.L.L.W.
• Frank Lloyd Wright
Taliesin • Spring-Green
Wisconsin Telephone 110
February 2nd. 1932.

[pc ts&ms lmp]

---

1 Norman N. Rice (1903–1985), American architect, writer, and educator.
2 Ellen Wijdeveld, wife of Hendricus Theodorus Wijdeveld.

[SENT TO LEWIS MUMFORD]

Mr. Norman N. Rice
c/o T. Square Club Journal,
Philadelphia, Pa.

My dear Norman Rice:

Your article in the *T. Square Club* was so well written and your point so well taken that I felt impelled to send you the enclosed.[1]

Sincerely Yours,

January 12th. 1932

[cc ts flwa]

1 Wright, "To the Neuter."

4002 LOCUST STREET
LONG ISLAND CITY, N.Y.

6 FEBRUARY 1932

Dear F.L.W.:

Your letters came the day before yesterday: they gave me much to think about, and I have been thinking hard ever since.

First: as to what most immediately concerns me, the suggestion as to whether Sophie and I would be willing to lead the Taliesin Fellowship. I am warmed by the honor and confidence and all that they imply: so, too, is Sophie: but much as I would like to be near you and to work with you, the job is outside my range and powers. I am now in the midst of a book: there are four or five other books inside of me, kicking around and waiting for their chance to be born: and, as you know, though we both are men, gestation is a good large job in itself, and necessarily everything else must take second place to it.[1] Even were I empty at the moment, as sometimes happens between births, I would seriously doubt my capacities, at least in the present stage of my life and experience: my quiet student's life is not the best sort of preparation for such leadership. I am grateful, then, but I must say No.

As to whether Wijdeveld is the right man for the job, that is another question. I had a few hours with him in the city here, no more: he seemed to have plenty of intelligence and understanding and enthusiasm, but I have no notion of how he would wear. It seems to me that the person who would have so many practical responsibilities as the leader should probably be an American: so that he will not be forced to waste his time acquiring all sorts of little matters of common knowledge, matters which would during the first few years divert his attention from the main task a little and perhaps cause irritation or friction. If you have any doubts at all about Wijdeveld I think that the fairest thing, even at this late stage of your relations, would be to call it off. Unless you yourself can close your eyes and say Go Ahead both your position and the leader's would be too delicate a one to remain in

---

1 Lewis Mumford, *Technics and Civilization* (New York: Harcourt, Brace and Company, 1934). Volume 1 of The Renewal of Life.

stable equilibrium any length of time. Wijdeveld would probably make a fine associate: but unless I misread your own sentiments, the burden of his being a leader would fall too heavily on both of you. There would be so many things in which he would have to be initiated.

Is there no one in Meiklejohn's school who has the right capacities? He should be between thirty and forty-five, I think: happily married and fairly well set on his own road: but that road should be one of personal contacts, the teacher's or administrator's, not the scholar's or the creative artist's.

As for the so called International Style: it is a dreadful phrase, since architecture is architecture and never, except in a bastard form, a style: so I share your irritation over it, and I sympathize with your disgust over the numerous neurotic and gutless young men, who have seized on the cliches and externalities of the new architecture, and made them their own. But the work itself is often much better than the words that are used about it: I have never thought seriously of Le Corbusier's talents as an architect, for his designs are as weak as his soul itself is arid: but both Van der Rohe and Oud seem to me to have some of the heart of the matter in them, and the fact that the Modern Museum show is a mixed one, with both good and bad stuff in it, seems to me almost inevitable, given the actual state of taste and knowledge and the limitations that dog even the best selection: I don't see how the good work can possibly suffer by juxtaposition with the insincere and the second-rate. But while the phrase international style emphasizes all the wrong things architecturally, I think it is a fine sign that men o[f] good will all over the world are beginning to face life in the same way, and to seek similar means of expressing it and focussing it: without such consciousness, your own work would not have been such a powerful influence in Europe. I am all for that common spirit, although I reject any little box of tags and labels that the pedants may construct for themselves and affix to the architecture. No one can be merely an American any longer, any more than he can be merely a New Yorker: we shall all be at each other's throats, and have neither civilization [n]or culture left, unless we become increasingly conscious of our common tasks and our common interests: this for architecture as well as anything else. The new architecture in Europe does tend toward communism: the Nazis in Germany are aware of this, and threaten to tear it all down, in favor of a brummagem Niebelungen architecture, at the same time that they castrate the Jews and bomb the communists: but the communism seems to me to grow inevitably out of the inescapable conditions of our lives today in communities. I have stated this as well as I know how in my introduction to Housing in the Museum catalog. Such individualism as we shall develop must now be expressed through the collective enterprise: there is real scope for it here, and as we humanize industry and reorient our whole culture towards life, the ground for a genuine organic architecture will be prepared. To secure more life, fuller leafing, a richer efflorescence, when that time comes, we must at the beginning, which is now, prune the whole plant right down to the stem: hence this sense of bareness, of sterility, which the gutless may out of their impotence look upon as a fine and a final thing: to me, on the other hand, it is just the pre-condition of new growth, a growth which will bring us, in communities, to the point of expression you have reached in your individual work. The Great City is doomed: I agree with you there: but life in communities will go on; and true individualism has nothing to fear from that growth. We must at least have the advantages of communism before we have anything humanly richer and more varied than what is implied in communism. Capitalism could favor an organic architecture only by way of escape: communism will favor it directly by way of growth.

These, then, are our differences and agreements. I can subscribe heartily to the credo you have written as the foundation of the Taliesin Fellowship: only, instead of city, I should write: the city of the past. The new city will be part again of its region and countryside; and the new countryside itself will not be segregated from the currents of thought and culture, which the city has monopolized for itself in the past. . . .

Now as to your exhibition. I do not alas! know Mrs. H.P. Whitney or anyone connected with her museum. If she is connected with the College Art Association, or if you know anyone there, that would be the most convenient means of getting the exhibit shown around the country: again, I have no connection with the directors there, but I know that they have an excellent system for routing around work. But you must try to come to New York soon yourself. I will meanwhile see if I can get hold of anybody who is competent to help you here. What about using the New School gallery? There is also a possibility of showing at the Brooklyn Museum: they are not as deeply stuck in the mud as the Metropolitan. You should be on hand in New York when your book comes out: indeed, your publishers ought on their own hook to invite you here and throw a party.[2]

I spent such a busy winter that I finally came down with a frightful cold last time I was in Dartmouth and have spent the last two weeks in the first spell of idleness I have had in a year and a half. The pleasure of merely dilly-dallying is enormous: I sort out vast masses of paper and rubbish, renew my youth, visit old friends, walk about the city, drink enormous quantities of sociable tea and coffee, go to bed early, and am happy. Sophie and Geddes are both busy with school, and every time I cancel a lecture or an article I feel as if I were getting a new lease on life! On the whole, the winter has been kinder to me than it has been to most people: the caprice of heaven. Catherine Bauer has been writing captions for the housing section and she tells me that the people at the museum, from Hitchcock down, are lost in admiration of your Mesa model. I have still to see it: that will come next Monday.

In the meanwhile, believe me

Affectionately yours
[signed]
Lewis

P.S. I see in glancing back over my proposal for a leader[,] I really suggested a different type of man than you had in mind. Don't you think there is something to be said for this: creative people are usually rotten in the details of administration, unless they cease to be creative: the impulse in all that concerns architecture and craftsmanship should come from you and the associates, it seems to me: and there is need for a kindly human being to grease the wheels and keep things going and attend to the practical routine. I should be afraid to mix up these two functions.

[ts flwa]

---

2 Wright, *An Autobiography*.

[C. FEBRUARY–MARCH 1932]

4002 LOCUST STREET
LONG ISLAND CITY

Dear F. L. W.:

Allan Twichell is a friend of mine: an able and serious young architect.[1] I heartily commend him to you; for you have much to give him and I think he has the capacity to use it.

Faithfully,
[signed]
Lewis

[ms flwa]

1 Allan Twichell, American architect.

4002 LOCUST ST.
LONG ISLAND CITY

2 MARCH 1932

Dear FLW:

My Chicago lecture fell through: so I shan't come out after all & instead I hope to see you here again at the end of March.

Have you thought of Ralph Pearson as a possible leader of the school[?][1] He is the only person who comes to my mind who meets all the abstract requirements with anything like fullness.

He is at the New School, & if you have not already done so, you should talk to him while you are here & size him up.

Warmly,
[signed]
Lewis

[ms flwa]

---

1 Ralph M. Pearson (1883–1958), American educator.

Mr. Lewis Mumford,
4002 Locust Street,
Long Island City,
New York.

Dear Lewis:

Taliesin was set back by the failure of the Chicago date. We had all counted on having you here.

Enclosed is the next to finished "Taliesin Fellowship" prospectus. I like your suggestion of Pearson but perhaps not as a leader but as an associate. Will see him when I get to N.Y. the last week in March.

I have gone after little Dr. A. Meiklejohn. He seems keen but doesn't know if he can do it. I tell him he can if he will just be himself. Your suggestion that the leader need not be a performer took this line with me. He should be a philosopher with some experience in educational work, broad enough to grasp the whole and personality of a kind to lead the flock. Doctor A. is as nearly these things as anyone I know.

Here is real experiment for him if he is truly a pioneer.

I should help him in every way possible and not get in the way. What do you think of him?

Faithfully,

March 19th. 1932.

[cc ts flwa]

[TELEGRAM]

APRIL 11 [1932] 12 P.M.

TO FRANK LLOYD WRIGHT

MUMFORD LUNCHEON THIS THURSDAY[;] PLEASE RUSH LAUREL[.]

AUDAC[1]

[flwa]

1 American Union of Decorative Artists and Craftsmen.

Mr. Nathan G. Horwitt
c.o. Audac
38 East 53rd Street, New York City

"Bon Voyage"
To Lewis Mumford—

Laurels are singularly becoming to Lewis Mumford—, the man Audacs honors itself by honoring, here today.

I should be "sitting in" to add my best to the laurels he already wears were there any money left in the world I inhabit—because I see in him the foremost constructive critic of American culture.

His is the nearest mind to Emerson's that we possess and the mind most likely to interpret to our country its own neglected ideals.

He is not afraid.

Nor will his social sense betray his sense of beauty because in the heart of him he is a creative artist, before all.

All America will be proud to call him "hers" before his day is done or her sun has set.

He is young in years and he is young in spirit.

He is strong and brave.

He is honest beneath and with his prowess and his laurels.

Anyone might say of Lewis as Napoleon said of Goethe—"here is a man."

It has been said that Lewis discovered me.

If he did, I am proud of his company.

I should have had more faith in myself discovered by him than by any pilot that sails the uncharted seas of our troubled twilight—be it dawn or be it eve.

During the next ten years we will know whether our culture is the twilight of dawn or the twilight of evening. If Lewis Mumford's work continues as it has begun, it will be sunrise and not sunset.

Audac! His health!

And may he return with more riches of the same kind.

To him a good voyage and a safe return to us all.

[signed]
Frank Lloyd Wright
Taliesin, April 11. 1932.

[pc ts&ms lmp, presented to Lewis Mumford]

[C. JUNE 1932]

(CO AMERICAN EXPRESS CO: BERLIN TILL 20 JUNE)
FRANKFURT-AM-MAIN

Dear FLW:

I have been in Europe for five weeks, and the words of your letter to Audac are still ringing in my ears, and making them blush and burn. Your letter was a benison indeed: after the last confused and hectic weeks in New York a calm settled down, my eyes and ears became keen and eager again; and since I landed I have had a better time traveling than I had ever known in Europe, or anywhere else, before. I cross my fingers & wonder how it happened—and then I remember your letter. And your book, too: the reading of that was a completion and a fulfillment of all that my admiration for your work and our all-too-brief moments together had given me: it is a living classic, worthy to be put beside your buildings.[1] I trust things have been going well with you & yours: at least, the flowers must come out in Taliesin & the beans must be sprouting now. Every now & then I have pangs for American earth, even though Europe has been giving me much, much to see, still more to think about.

In architecture, about a tenth of the modern work is genuinely good: I came across a farm-house and barn by Häring, near Lübeck, which would have delighted you, and the new subway stations in Berlin are pretty fine—as is much of the old steel-engineering.[2] But there is much formula, much dogma, much paper—their stuff, along with what is good & sound: and the show in reality is not as brave in fact as it seems in literature.[3] Still: people are better housed than they ever were before: the small gardens are becoming more numerous: the parks and sports stadia are becoming more numerous too: the realities of life are beginning to shine through. . . . Sophy may come here to join me in July—if I can bear being another month away from my little boy! But at all events I shall be back in August. A word from you, if you have the time, will be welcome.

---

1 Wright, *An Autobiography*.

2 Hugo Häring (1882–1958), German architect.

3 *Modern Architecture: International Exhibition*.

Affectionately,
[signed]
Lewis

P.S. My friend Behrendt in Berlin, a devout admirer of yours, concludes his still unpublished book on modern architecture with a chapter: Wright or Le Corbusier? You misunderstood his review last spring I think: he is on your side.

[ms flwa]

1933–1939

Letters from the remainder of the decade are infrequent, as Wright and Mumford become absorbed in major projects: Wright in the Taliesin Fellowship and the construction of its new winter headquarters, Taliesin West, as well as the design of "Fallingwater" and the S. C. Johnson & Sons Headquarters; Mumford in The Renewal of Life, a four-volume study of Western civilization that urges an end to technological determinism and a return to organic balance in modern life. A major disagreement erupts over Wright's Broadacre City project, which is exhibited in Rockefeller Center in 1935 and reviewed by Mumford in the *New Yorker*. Wright proposes rehousing the American population at low densities in single-family houses, while Mumford promotes somewhat higher densities in single- and multi-family residential units on the European model.

Mr. Lewis Mumford: 4002 Locust Street: Long Island C.

My dear Lewis:

For a long time, ever since your spirited and inspiring letter from Germany which reached me too late for immediate answer, I thought, I've wanted to see you and talk with you.

And a week or so ago somebody handed me *Harper's* with your appraisal of the book—which made me happy indeed.[1] As you probably know, your clean-cut opinions mean more to me than any criticisms I know. So imagine my satisfaction last time in New York—it is long ago—I made a hasty attempt to connect with you at the old address but getting no response was whirled away into the vortex and soon out. Betty Bauer gave me a word of you—through Catherine, I believe.[2]

Betty is in the trenches in blue overalls—and all outdoors "sweating" like a young colt. There is no "gesture" there but action. Much of the "New Yorker" has been shed with the perspiration. Hers is a good spirit here. Although something of a temptation to some of the boys here she carries herself, I should say, very well, all things considered.

Though I write little I think of you often and wish you might come out toward spring and be "leader" for a week or two. Let me know when to arrange it? Give my best to your little family—and remember me to Catherine Bauer. The work is slowly getting into form here. I am not hurrying it believing the thing should "grow" and the accretions of various sorts be as spontaneous or "volunteer" as possible.

The matter grows more encouraging every day.

My best to you Lewis—

Affectionately,

Spring Green Wis

January 1 [1933]: Frank Lloyd Wright

[cc ts flwa]

---

1 Lewis Mumford, "What Has 1932 Done for Literature?" *Atlantic Monthly* 150 (December 1932): 761–767; this review essay covered Wright's *An Autobiography*. Wright erred in his reference to the journal.

2 Elizabeth Bauer (1911–1998), American writer, curator, member of the Taliesin Fellowship, and sister of Catherine Bauer.

4002 LOCUST ST.
LONG ISLAND CITY

20 JANUARY 1933

Dear FLW:

I was sorry to miss you when you were last in town: but I have thought of you often and have fastened avidly on all the friendly reports I have heard of the Fellowship. Its existence is a miracle in an otherwise sordid year: and I wish I could join you this spring. But I have at last settled down to my book and I don't expect to raise my eyes from it, or give any real thought to anything else, much before the harvest is in—if indeed it be finished then.[1]

If you come East this spring, do try to let me know in advance. I have a hundred things to talk to you about: but this letter comes at the end of a long day at the Library: so it is, in reality, just a promise of a livelier letter at a better time.

Sophy joins me in warm greetings to you both.

[signed]
Lewis

[ms flwa]

---

1 Mumford, *Technics and Civilization*.

Mr. Lewis Mumford: 4002 Locust Street: Long Island City

Dear Mr. Mumford:

Thank you for your letter to Mr. Wright which I have forwarded to him in California where he is at present lecturing. Mr. Wright will be in New York March 15th when he lectures for the Institute of Arts and Sciences in Brooklyn.

I am sending under separate cover a copy of the new prospectus of the Fellowship.

Sincerely,

Karl E. Jensen: Spring Green Wisconsin: Taliesin: Jan 23:33[1]

[cc ts flwa]

1 Karl E. Jensen (1860–1951), secretary to Frank Lloyd Wright in the early 1930s.

AMENIA, NEW YORK

2 JULY 1933

Dear F.L.W.:

It is long since I have heard from you and seen you: but I can only hope that you have been as busy and as happy as I have been during the last few months. Since the beginning of June I have been up here writing my book, and if the days only remained as happy as the last month has been, I would wish them to go on a thousand years without more change than they themselves hold—although that is not little.[1] The book goes well: but it also is becoming enormous. I feel like repeating Melville's call for fifty fast-writing youths to help me get it all down, and I can see plainly that my work is cut out for me during the next three or four years, merely to finish up adequately what I have begun in this first interpretation of the machines. Some of the theses, will, I know, be very close to your own heart and mind, for I am demonstrating how the machine had its origin out of the denial of the organic, how it throve and came to dominate the organic, and how now we are on the point of—in the midst of?—reversing this process, so that the organic will once more dominate the machine. To lay a strong foundation for this, and to build on it a firm and solid and comely book is no easy job, partly because so much of the necessary history has been neglected, and partly because so many of the alleged facts about the development of the machine are misleading, and even false. But if the book is as good as I now have reason to think it will be, it will give a strong impulse in the direction it anticipates and prophesies. When will it be finished? If I work hard and unremittingly, I may have the manuscript done by next January: so I now plan. At earliest publication will be next spring.

I have just received word from Walter Curt Behrendt that, despite the fact that he is a jew [*sic*] and despite the change that has taken place in all the publishing houses, the Propylaen Verlag is going to publish his book on the modern dwelling house.[2] You have, he tells me, handsomely met his request for photographs of your work: but he still lacks

1 Mumford, *Technics and Civilization*.

2 As noted, this work was evidently not published.

photos of the Roberts Cottage and of your own Taliesin, and the latter is particularly important for him.[3] I have both of these myself; but they are in storage and I won't be able to get at them till the end of the summer; so I wonder if you have any prints to send him. He is not merely a very excellent critic, but he is one of the few people in Europe today who understands thoroughly what you are doing; and he has a lengthy chapter in his book on your work and on its significance both in the past and for the future. His address is Hanauerstrasse 45, Berlin-Wilmersdorf.

What of your own work? A line would be welcome.

[signed]
Lewis

[ts flwa]

3 Frank Lloyd Wright, Isabel Roberts Residence, River Forest, Illinois, 1908.

Mr. Lewis Mumford,
Amenia, New York

My dear Lewis:

Tardy, yes, but there's a reason.

Immersed above the limit of communication or is it below? That is all.

I think of you with affection and esteem—with faith in you and your forthcoming book. Your passionate devotion to work ought to get something, not only healthy, born but something vivid it seems to me.

A note from C.B. indicates her interest and working energy.[1] The Fellowship grows slowly as things organic must. Have had no outside help yet from any quarter—but the spirit of the lads and lassies encourages me to keep on.

If we round out the coming winter, and I guess we will, it all ought to be easier for me and better for them.

I've changed the original plan a good deal because I was near to "institution" in the thing myself. I've backed away—keeping the whole more spontaneous and the road wide open. I'll tell you more about it when I arrive at Columbia to lecture November 20th.[2] As usual those I expect to "come along" do not and from unexpected sources comes what we have. This may be owing to bad judgement on my part or to natural human perversity.

I suppose you could get to us for a while to give us a lift. Anyhow, what does it matter in the long run.

My best to yours,

Faithfully yours,
[signed]
F.L.L.W.
Frank Lloyd Wright,
Taliesin, Spring Green: Wis.
October 18th. 1933.

[ts jscl]

---

1 Catherine Bauer.

2 Columbia University, New York City.

4002—44 ST.
LONG ISLAND CITY

4 MAY 1934

Dear F. L. W.:

I am too broke at the moment to order the new monograph: but if "Technics" makes out all right I'll send my order in in June.[1] Meanwhile I'm sending you a copy of that weighty book.

Warmly,
[signed]
Lewis

[ms flwa]

---

1 Frank Lloyd Wright, *Taliesin* (Spring Green, WI: Taliesin, 1934); Mumford, *Technics and Civilization*.

Lewis Mumford: Amenia: New York

Dear Lewis:

Fair enough. And we can have your coveted signature on the enclosed blank on the basis of barter. The book for the monograph?

You would have had the monograph anyway and I should have bought the book but I wanted to keep faith with the "no complimentary copies." I see such good reports of the book and believe it is going "to carry you." I shall read it sure of gratification. The world needs what you can give it. I am glad you are to the fore with good work at this time.

Wish you could find your way out here with Sophie and Geddes and rusticate with us for a month or two. What are you doing this summer?

Faithfully—as always,
Frank Lloyd Wright
Taliesin: Spring Green: Wisconsin: May the Seventh [1934]

[cc ts flwa]

[INSCRIPTION IN *Technics and Civilization*]

To Frank Lloyd Wright who made the difference between the mechanical and the organic visible in architecture—and so helped to initiate the biotechnic phase

[signed]
Lewis Mumford
21 May 1934

[ms flwa]

Lewis Mumford: Amenia: New York

Dear Lewis:

I've neglected writing to thank you for the book until I could say something intelligent concerning it. But I've yet only partly read it owing to the squeeze on the general cook and bottle-washer of the Taliesin Fellowship, which wishes often that you could come out and put in a couple of weeks—"you" meaning wife and son too—and work with us. You would enjoy it almost as much as we would.

Your book is important but you would get something important out of us as we would out of you. Think it over. The book is, needless to say—great work.

Faithfully,
Frank Lloyd Wright,
Taliesin: Spring Green: Wisconsin: August 6th, 1934

[cc ts flwa]

4002—44 STREET
LONG ISLAND CITY

30 SEPTEMBER 1934

Dear F L W:

I hope some good wind will blow you East soon! After a fallow summer I'm back at work again. We grew the biggest cucumbers, Jerusalem artichokes & hollyhocks in Dutchess County; and Sophy is expecting a baby next May. So there!

All good wishes,
[signed]
Lewis

[ms flwa]

Lewis Mumford: Amenia: New York

Dear Lewis:

I've just read "Wright's City" in the *New Yorker* and find you trying rather hard to be nice to me.[1] At least so it seemed to me as I read. I am sorry we couldn't have gone into Broadacres a little more thoroughly because the main value of the whole thing save architecturally is quite missed in your criticism.[2]

I don't know what you can mean by preferring the German tenement and slum solution as preferable to the Broadacre's minimum house and maximum of space.

There can be no possible comparison between the two as privacy, light and air, living accommodations—or what have you—at $600.00.

Add to that, that the tenement unit in the rank and file in Broadacres becomes a complete individual little free-holding no less sightly and dignified in quality as an individual home than those near it having more as material resources and what have you?

I must confess, you puzzle me Lewis. When you have time (I suppose you have little enough)—please explain. Will you? You might teach me something I ought to know.

Affectionately,
[signed]
F.L.L.W.
Frank Lloyd Wright
Taliesin: Spring Green: Wisconsin
April 27th, 1935

[pc ts lmp]

1 Lewis Mumford, "The Sky Line: Mr. Wright's City; Downtown Dignity," *New Yorker* 11 (27 April 1935): 63–65.

2 Frank Lloyd Wright, Project for Broadacre City, 1934.

AMENIA, NEW YORK

25 JUNE 1935

Dear F.L.W. :

Your letter to me was written on the eve of Alison Jane's birth: that explains my long silence, or rather, accounts for it.[1] She is a fine girl, with a shapely and unaccountably nordic looking head, long legs, a healthy appetite and a placid disposition. Sophia has been magnificent through the whole business; so we are settling down to what ought, with good luck, be a good summer here.

As for that review of mine, like all the things I write in the *New Yorker* it touched only the surface; and I could not go into details, although there were plenty of things that I'd like to thresh out with you. Certainly I wasn't trying to be nice to you: there was no room for that, nor any need for the trying. The thing about which we fundamentally disagree is not what you put forward but what you reject. I think it is silly to lump all the good and bad things that have been done in European housing as a "slum solution." You can only do this by holding dogmatically that anything except a single family house on its own broad acre of land is a slum.

For me, on the other hand, the type of city you have so admirably worked out in Broadacre City is one of half a dozen potential urban types that we can develop in order to achieve the maximum possibilities of life. My own scheme of life has a place in it for Römerstadt as well as for Broadacre City, because concentration, when not pushed to the point of congestion, offers certain possibilities of intercourse that dispersion doesn't.[2] In practice, I have had experience of both of them at their best: the winter in Sunnyside and the summer in this hamlet and township which has in broad outlines, derived from the older pattern of agricultural life, most of the characteristics of your developed design.[3] Our own holding of land here, an acre and a half, is ample for

1 Alison Jane Mumford (1935–1993), American artist, educator, and daughter of Lewis and Sophia Mumford.

2 Ernst May, Römerstadt Housing Estate, near Frankfurt, Germany, 1926.

3 Stein and Wright, Sunnyside Gardens, Long Island City, Queens, 1924–1928, where the Mumfords maintained their city residence.

both vegetable garden and flowers; and I am even now planting an orchard. Unlike Catherine Bauer, I don't reject your Broadacre City as a romantic dream; but by the same token I don't think it is a universal solution.

This is apart from the particular question of housing. I flatly doubt that anyone can design a house containing the elemental modern decencies that can be built for $600 today; and if it could be done, I am not sure that it should; for an ideal scheme of living should not be based on such wide disparities of income as you picture in Broadacre City: it would be better to design a more spacious minimum house and level incomes toward a better common mean. Economically speaking—apart from the fact that you guarantee a minimum amount of land—the pattern of Broadacre City too closely resembles that of a contemporary suburb with a few light manufacturing industries.

Perhaps you'll see better what I am driving at—and in the meanwhile I'll try zealously to understand better what you are driving at—when I get my next book finished.[4] I shall spend the rest of the summer mulling over it, and I hope to start work on the manuscript toward the beginning of autumn.

Sophie joins me in warm greetings.

Affectionately,
[signed]
Lewis

[ts flwa]

4 Lewis Mumford, *The Culture of Cities* (New York: Harcourt, Brace and Company, 1938). Volume 2 of The Renewal of Life.

Lewis Mumford
Amenia
New York

My dear Mr. Mumford:

I was very sorry that my stay in New York was cut short so that I did not have the privilege of meeting and talking with you. I was there on a mission for Mr. Wright in terms of the Taliesin Fellowship and I would like to have had the opportunity to tell you in person about the work we are doing and to convey to you Mr. Wright's great wish—and members of the group around him here, as well—that you come to visit us soon and for as long a time as possible, bringing your family. Mr. Wright, I think, feels that "urbanity" and urbanism might be getting the better of you and wants to reassure himself that New York is not the same poison to you as to all other men of genius.

Mr. Wright is hard at work with the Fellowship on several projects which would surely interest you—houses designed for eight different states, several in process of construction. It is important now that Taliesin's field of activity be extended even further. We have not found many unselfish enough to come our way—yet. In fact we have asked but few.

We are all hoping that sometime this summer you may be in the middle west and will make Taliesin your objective. We could send down and bring you and Dr. Walter Curt Behrendt and your families for a week or so if you cared to have us do so. We have a comfortable fleet of cars of several types from station wagon to coupe.

Mr. Wright would write himself but he has suffered a painful accident—being tossed from the road grader while making a new road—couple of ribs broken—neck wrenched—leg twisted—but is around again now and will no doubt write to you himself—soon.

Sincerely yours,
[signed]
Eugene Masselink[1]
Secretary to Frank Lloyd Wright
Taliesin: Spring Green: Wisconsin
July first, 1936

[pc tc lmp]

---

1 Eugene Masselink (1910–1962), artist, business manager, and secretary to Frank Lloyd Wright from the mid-1930s.

MUMFORD
AMENIA, NEW YORK

9 JULY 1936

Dear Eugene Masselink:

I was grieved to miss you in New York, and was on the point of writing you an apology when your letter came: but I was in the midst of a spate of work, from which I have scarcely lifted my head: hence my silence. If your coming up here had been feasible, you would have seen that metropolitanism and urbanism have been far from getting the better of me: this is a very lush part of the country, not unlike that of Taliesin, I should judge, in its contours, and though this farmhouse was built by other hands a hundred years ago, the re-making of it, and the planting of the garden, have been ours: a little detached unit, as it were, of Broadacre City! My book on the city will be much closer to FLW's heart than he probably suspects: the difference being that whereas he dismisses megalopolis with a wave of his hand, I take it apart, stone by stone, from foundation to pinnacle.[1] But when we come to new structures, as he well knows, I am on his side: not on that of the ticker-men and the white-tapeworms, nor on that symbolized by Le Corbusier. As for the trip to Taliesin, I am still looking forward to it, as I have been looking forward these many years: the difficulty consists in joining time and money and opportunity, for though at one point or another I have had one of these in my possession, all three of them together have so far been lacking. My family doesn't transport easily: and my work is even harder to transport: that is what keeps me tied here—that, and the fact that my roots are sunk deep here. But a short visit alone is a prime item on my program for the next year; and as soon as it becomes possible I'll quickly let you know. In the meanwhile, please tell FLW how sorry I am about his accident and how affectionately Sophy and I think of him from time to time, letter or no letter.

With all good wishes,

Faithfully yours
[signed]
Lewis Mumford

[ts flwa]

---

1 Mumford, *The Culture of Cities*.

Mr. Lewis Mumford
Amenia
New York

Dear Mr. Mumford:

Thank you for your very pleasant letter. Mr. Wright was glad to hear of your work in your own hilly "Broadacre City unit." He is disappointed that you aren't able to make the trip to Taliesin this summer but anticipates—as do all of us—the promised visit for next year.

If you would happen to know Mr. Paley, President of Columbia Broadcasting System or any other big men in that company in New York we would appreciate learning about it.[1] Anton Rovinsky of N. Y., pianist at Taliesin during the summer months, is informed that they are planning to build a large building in the city (this information on the "aside").[2] Knowing one of the Columbia officials he is working to push interest in this direction.

Although Mr. Wright has never and would never go out to get a "job," I can see no reason why these gentlemen and others like them should not be educated so to see for themselves the significance and structural beauty an organic building in New York would have for America.

Sincerely yours,
Eugene Masselink
Secretary to Frank Lloyd Wright
Taliesin: Spring Green: Wisconsin
July 16th, 1936

[cc ts flwa]

1 William S. Paley (1901–1990), president of the Columbia Broadcasting System (CBS).
2 Anton Rovinsky (1895–1966), musician.

MUMFORD
AMENIA, NEW YORK

18 JULY 1936

Dear Eugene Masselink:

Just a hasty line to say that I don't know Paley nor any other person in the Columbia Broadcasting System; but of course if I by accident get a chance to put in a timely word, I'll spring to the occasion. It would be marvellous to have Wright do such a building. . . . Rain is falling again here: a pleasant sound in the gray twilight: I trust plenty of it has fallen onto Taliesin, too, and that all manner of good things come with it and start to life and grow.

Ever yours
[signed]
Lewis Mumford

P.S. Since you say nothing about FLW's health I trust he's whole once more.

[ts&ms flwa]

MUMFORD
AMENIA, NEW YORK

28 AUGUST 1937

Dear F.L.W.:

I am at last finishing up my book on The Culture of Cities, which I hope to have published early next spring; and I have reached the stage of gathering photographs for reproduction. Is a photograph of the Broadacre City Model available? When it was reproduced in the *Record* it seemed reasonably clear and intelligible.[1] The book has reached monumental proportions by now: and ironically enough, one of my last chapters is on The Death of the Monument! In the act of writing the final sections on the forms of the future, I have found myself closer to you in thought and outlook than perhaps ever before: perhaps because I have now spent almost two consecutive years on the land.[2] Next January I expect to be out in Minneapolis, giving a lecture: an engagement I accepted because it gave me some hope of seeing you at Taliesin, if you have not by then hived off to a warmer spot. Sophy joins me in warm greetings to you and your wife.

Ever yours
[signed]
Lewis

[ts flwa]

---

1 Frank Lloyd Wright, "Broadacre City: A New Community Plan," *Architectural Record* 77 (April 1935): 243–254.
2 The Mumfords moved permanently to Amenia in 1936.

MR. LEWIS MUMFORD: AMENIA: NEW YORK

Dear Mr. Mumford:

Since receiving your letter we have been getting material together on Broadacre City for you to see and are sending it herewith together with a photograph of the model which we would like to have returned as soon as you have finished using it.

The literature with the photograph is to be used in our next issue of the monograph *TALIESIN* and since it gives a rather complete survey of Broadacre City[,] Mr. Wright wanted you to have it to acquaint you more thoroughly with what was behind the whole project.[1]

With Mr. Wright's—and Taliesin's—best wishes,

Sincerely yours,
Eugene Masselink
Secretary to Frank Lloyd Wright
Taliesin: Spring Green: Wisconsin
October 2nd, 1937

[cc ts flwa]

1 *Taliesin* was private publication of the Taliesin Fellowship, edited by Frank Lloyd Wright. This particular issue was Vol.1 No.1 October 1940.

MUMFORD
AMENIA, NEW YORK

4 OCTOBER 1937

Dear Mr. Masselink:

Thanks for your help. I've read the enclosed pages with renewed pleasure: and I will return the photograph as soon as I can get it back from the photo-engravers.

With all good wishes & thanks,

Faithfully yours,
[signed]
Lewis Mumford

[ms flwa]

Mr. Lewis Mumford: Amenia: New York

Dear Lewis:

Your *New Yorker* piece on genuine bootleg shows we aren't dead yet.[1] Keep it up.

Wish'd you was here . . .

Frank Lloyd Wright
August 10th, 1939

[cc ts flwa]

1 Lewis Mumford, "The Sky Line in Flushing: Genuine Bootleg," *New Yorker* 15 (29 July 1939): 38–41.

1941

Wright is the subject of a major exhibition at the Museum of Modern Art in winter 1940–1941; soon after, *Frank Lloyd Wright on Architecture* is published. Politics, which have so far remained in the background of the correspondence, move to the fore in an impassioned exchange of letters in June. Mumford, incensed over Wright's anti-war sentiments, renounces the architect's friendship. Wright's reply completes the breakdown in relations. A ten-year lapse in the correspondence ensues.

LEWIS MUMFORD
AMENIA, NEW YORK

2 APRIL 1941

Dear Frank Lloyd Wright:

I am shocked over the fact that the Chicago Theological Seminary intends to destroy the Robie house.[1] It is as complete a piece of vandalism as the proposal to run a new traffic artery through the Auditorium Building.[2] I am herewith sending a protest to the President of the Chicago Theological Seminary and I shall try to get others to join in.

It seems years since we last met, and probably it is. One of the penalties of living up here is that I am never on hand to catch you when you are passing through New York.

From all the evidence of your recent creative exuberance that the Modern Museum Exhibition showed, I gather that you have been in the best of health and that all the juices of you are still flowing harmoniously.[3]

As you perhaps know I have spent a good part of the last couple of years endeavoring to awaken the country to the need for attacking Hitler before he has a chance to carry through even a small part of his program for enslaving the world. Now that the country seems at least half awake to this danger, and has abandoned the silly illusion that it can come to terms with Hitler, or insulate itself by mere defence measures from Hitlerism, I am settling back into the writing of the third volume of my series.[4]

With all good wishes and hopes for an early meeting,

Ever yours,
[signed]
Lewis

[ts flwa]

---

1 Frank Lloyd Wright, Frederick C. Robie Residence, Chicago, 1908.

2 Adler and Sullivan, Auditorium Building, Chicago, 1887–1890.

3 *Two Great Americans: Frank Lloyd Wright and D.W. Griffith*, exhibition, Museum of Modern Art, New York, 13 November 1940 to 5 January 1941.

4 Lewis Mumford, *The Condition of Man* (New York: Harcourt, Brace and Company, 1944). Volume 3 of The Renewal of Life.

[ONE OF NUMEROUS FORM LETTERS SENT TO SUPPORTERS]

Dear Lewis:

Thank you for your help. I wish I could see more of you this coming summer—somehow. Why not at Taliesin?

Sincerely,
Frank Lloyd Wright
April 14th, 1941

[cc ts flwa]

LEWIS MUMFORD
AMENIA, NEW YORK

20 APRIL 1941

Dear FLW:

I want very much to visit you at Taliesin; and if you are there in June when I come by from California, I will. But I hope that by that time your political views have caught up with your architecture. War is of course no antidote to Hitler: but unless we have the guts and the intelligence to fight him now we will never have the chance to develop an antidote. Are you still in the Neville Chamberlain period? Period politics are as bad as period architecture.

Ever yours,
[signed]
Lewis

[ms flwa]

Mr. Lewis Mumford
Amenia, New York

Dear Lewis:

We will be glad to see you this summer whenever the spirit moves you to stop with us.

It is a real pain to me to find ourselves in disagreement. I know little of politics. What opinions I hold are based only upon principles I apprehend. So I am sure we have no quarrel outside what expedients to employ.

Faithfully as always,
Frank Lloyd Wright
April 29th, 1941

[cc ts flwa]

AMENIA, NEW YORK

30 MAY 1941

My dear Frank Lloyd Wright:

A few days ago I corrected proofs on a brief tribute to you and your work which will come out next week in the *New Yorker*, by way of reviewing Gutheim's collection of your writings.[1] I am glad that I wrote those words; for they were called forth by a man whose work and spirit I have long admired and will continue to admire.

Yesterday, however, there came to me a broadside, with your name at the bottom of it; and I have read and re-read the words in it with growing astonishment: with astonishment over its crassness, with incredulity over its blindness, with anger over its shameless defeatism, and with indignation over its callous lack of moral perception.[2] Did <u>you</u> write that broadside—or your worst enemy?

In this strange tirade you use the word gangster, not to characterize Hitler and his followers, but to castigate those who would fight to the death rather than see Hitler's "new order" prevail in any part of the earth. You hurl reproaches against the system of empire, meaning by this only the British Empire, an empire that widened the area of justice and freedom and peace: but you have not a word to say against the Slave Empire that Germany would set on its ruins and extend far beyond its present borders.

In plain words, you are ready to accept a world order based on totalitarian corruption and slavery and terrorism; but you are not man enough to state openly the only terms on which Americans could purchase peace or security in such a world—namely by active cooperation. Perhaps you believe in such cooperation? There is more than a hint of this in your statement.

On reflection, I find I have no reason to be astonished over your

---

1 Lewis Mumford, "The Sky Line: The Architecture of Power," *New Yorker* 17 (7 June 1941): 58–60; Frederick Gutheim.

2 Frank Lloyd Wright, "A Taliesin Square-Paper: A Nonpolitical Voice from our Democratic Minority," privately printed, 1941; reprinted as "Of What Use is a Great Navy with No Place to Hide?" in *Frank Lloyd Wright: Collected Writings, Volume 4, 1939–1949*, edited by Bruce Brooks Pfeiffer with an introduction by Kenneth Frampton (New York: Rizzoli in association with the Frank Lloyd Wright Foundation, 1994), 73–77.

defeatism, your moral callousness, or even your insufferable hypocrisy—"I love England." These are not the traits of the living Frank Lloyd Wright I will always admire. They are the marks of a dead man: the words carry the stench of such a putrefaction as can come only from the grave.

It is hard to lose a friend by his physical death; but it is even more painful to lose him by his spiritual death: above all at such a time as this, when one looked to Frank Lloyd Wright to be a leader of the fight for freedom, wherever it might be threatened, and a defender of democracy, in every country where men still were faithful to the ideals of humanity. Instead, you advocate a slave's safety, and a coward's withdrawal.

What a spectacle! You shrink into your selfish ego and urge America to follow you; you are willing to abandon to their terrible fate the conquered, the helpless, the humiliated, the suffering: you carefully refrain from offending, if only by a passing reference, those Nazi overlords to whom in your heart you, like Lindbergh, have already freely given the fruits of victory.[3] In short: you have become a living corpse: a spreader of active corruption. You dishonor all the generous impulses you once ennobled. Be silent! lest you bring upon yourself some greater shame.

[signed]
Lewis Mumford

Mr. Frank Lloyd Wright
Taliesin
Spring Green
Wisconsin.

[ts&ms flwa][4]

3 Charles A. Lindbergh (1902–1974), American aviator and political activist.
4 Published as Lewis Mumford, "Frank Lloyd Wright's Defeatism Aids Slave Empire—Mumford," *New Leader* 24 (14 June 1941): 8.

Frank Lloyd Wright's remodeled apartment interior, Plaza Hotel, New York, 1954.
Photograph © Pedro E. Guerrero. Frank Lloyd Wright Archives, 5532.0003.

Modern Architecture: International Exhibition, Museum of Modern Art, New York, February–March 1932. Interior view of Frank Lloyd Wright section, including the model of the Project for a House on the Mesa, Denver, Colorado, 1931. Museum of Modern Art Archives.

Model of the Project for a House on the Mesa, Denver, Colorado, 1931. Frank Lloyd Wright Archives, 3102.0017.

Model of the Project for Broadacre City, 1934. Photograph by Skot Weidemann, 1994. Frank Lloyd Wright Archives, 3402.0090. © 1994 Frank Lloyd Wright Foundation.

Sixty Years of Living Architecture, exhibition in temporary pavilion at future site of the Solomon R. Guggenheim Museum, New York, November 1953. Photograph © Pedro E. Guerrero. Frank Lloyd Wright Archives, 5314.0018.

Jean and Paul Hanna Residence ("Honeycomb House"), Palo Alto, California, 1935. View of living room. Sturtevant photographs. Frank Lloyd Wright Archives, 3701.0277.

Lloyd Lewis Residence, Libertyville, Illinois, 1939. View of living room. Photograph by Hedrich-Blessing. Chicago Historical Society; Frank Lloyd Wright Archives, 4008.0016.

Utagawa Hiroshige, *Kanda Temple in Snow*, c. mid-nineteenth century. Color woodblock print inscribed by Frank Lloyd Wright to Lewis Mumford. Estate of Lewis and Sophia Mumford.

Taliesin, Spring Green, Wisconsin, 1925. View of living room, 1937. Photograph by Hedrich-Blessing. Chicago Historical Society; Frank Lloyd Wright Archives, 2501.0234.

Taliesin West, Scottsdale, Arizona, 1937. View of drafting room, 1946. Photograph by Maynard Parker. Frank Lloyd Wright Archives, 3803.0040.

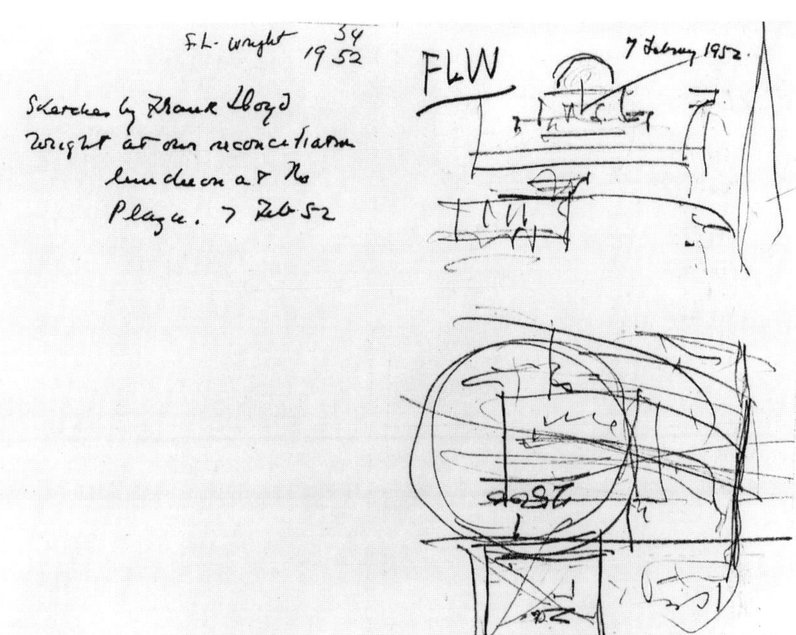

Frank Lloyd Wright, sketches of Wainwright Tomb, 7 February 1952. Lewis Mumford Papers, Annenberg Rare Book and Manuscript Library, University of Pennsylvania.

Louis H. Sullivan and Frank Lloyd Wright, Wainwright Tomb, Bellefontaine Cemetery, St. Louis, Missouri, 1892. Frank Lloyd Wright Archives, 7116.0077.

For Frank: with love:
The book that first
brought us together.

Lewis

Amenia, N.Y.
September 1955

Lewis Mumford, inscription in *Sticks and Stones*, rev. ed., Dover Publications, September 1955. Frank Lloyd Wright Archives, 1156.207.

My dear Lewis:

When, because of a difference of feeling and judgement, you can so shamelessly insult one who has trusted your sincerity, admired your ability, and praised you as a manly man, well, Lewis, I can understand your anguish and desire for revenge—but reactions such as yours are certainly not trustworthy when and wherever the welfare of this nation is at stake, as I believe it to be and as you say you believe it to be.

Be ashamed of yourself, Lewis. Some day—but take your time. I am human grass roots in the service of the culture of a beloved country. I can give you time.

For the same reason that I despise eclecticism and reaction I despise your attitude toward war and Empire. There is no good Empire; there never was a just war. I despise your attitude now as I despised "the setting-sun all Europe mistook for dawn." It was called the "Renaissance."

If going to war is now your way, you have never settled anything for yourself nor ever will for anyone else. Yours is the mind that would throw the dead cat back and forth across the backyard fence.

And I don't mean what you mean when I say "I love England." I love my England. You love yours. I hate master-empire or slave-empire. So my England is not your England and I am thankful.

You prate of culture, Lewis. Organic character is the basis of true greatness in that or in any individual or in any nation. War is the negation of all these potentialities now as ever and forever. You know that. And yet you wrote to me that you had been busy getting the United States ready to fight and having accomplished that to your satisfaction you were ready to go back and write another book.

Christ! Lewis, is it possible that you are unable to see your own hypocrisy? Why do you try to hide behind what you call mine?

No honest believer in truth or beauty in his right mind could do what you say you have done. Time will discover you a deserter. A traitor on a battle-field that did you honor only to discover in you a vengeful, conceited writer. Another writer out of ideas. The Chinese say it well: "He who runs out of ideas first strikes the first blow."

<u>You</u> standing with the frightened crowd for the time-cursed expedient! What a disappointment. And yet I could take it all from you because you are young and still be your friend if I believed you sincere in your anguish and in your desire for revenge. But you are not.

You prate of "downtrodden democracies" and of "defending

slaves," to justify your own rage and impotence. Why not honestly examine your own heart? What you would see there is what you accuse me of . . . hypocrisy.

Lewis, my young friend, one I liked to call up and talk to whenever I got to the great city, you, too, are yellow with this strange but ancient sickness of the soul.

The malady that has thrown down civilization after civilization by meeting force with force. Is meeting force with force the only way you see now? Then I am sorry for you—you amateur essayist on culture. It is not the only way I see. I—a builder—see that there is still a chance for democracy in this world and one on this continent just because the leaders of our culture are not all like Lewis Mumford, as he shows his teeth now.

Goodbye, Lewis, I shall read your "brief" in the *New Yorker* with shame. I shall read it knowing your real opinion is worthless whatever you may write.

Sincerely yours,
[signed]
Frank Lloyd Wright
Taliesin
Spring Green
Wisconsin
June 3rd, 1941

[pc ts lmp]

1946

Although five years have passed since Wright and Mumford last exchanged letters, the bond between them is not entirely dissolved. Mumford's letter to poet and writer John Gould Fletcher serves as a kind of interlude in the correspondence. In it, Mumford recapitulates with mixed emotions his feelings about Wright and the disagreement that led to their unfortunate break.

46 College Street: Hanover, New Hampshire: 10 April 1946

Dear John Gould Fletcher:[1]

Even the sight of your handwriting on the envelope gave me pleasure when your letter came; so you can imagine how much deeper was my response to your very generous words. The ability to write Gentlemen: You are Mad came at the end of six weeks I had spent doing the first draft of a brief memoir of my son: following him through his brief and tragic life, darkened as it was almost from the moment of his birth, I got from him the strength that was needed to overcome the paralysis that has afflicted us all.[2] Believe me: we are not alone in feeling as we do about the atomic bomb. Many of our countrymen are equally perturbed, and during the past month or so their voices have been growing in volume and in confidence. Sophia and I have spent most of our time the last six weeks attempting to give this widespread protest some more definite goal, along the lines of the enclosed petition. We have distributed some 1500 petitions; but since we have purposely kept the movement on a voluntary, decentralized basis we have no notion as to how it is prospering. No one form of action will probably be sufficient for the occasion; but all these separate trickles, though they seem to come to nothing, may eventually form a river and cut through the political landscape.

The questions you raise about Frank Lloyd Wright are for me very interesting ones. I have long reflected on them, though I have not yet given adequate expression in print to my answers. On the positive side, I should say he is one of the great architectural geniuses of our time; not merely that, but of any time. Such a fertile architectural imagination is hardly met with in any age: it takes one back to the kind of genius that encompassed the change from Romanesque building to high Gothic. He has more imagination in his little finger than most of his contemporaries have in their whole organism, and his combination of the poet and the engineer is a rare one, though the

1 John Gould Fletcher (1886–1950), American poet and critic.

2 Lewis Mumford, "Gentlemen: You Are Mad!" *Saturday Review of Literature* 29 (2 March 1946): 5–6; Lewis Mumford, *Green Memories: The Story of Geddes Mumford* (New York: Harcourt, Brace and Company, 1947). Geddes Mumford, a U.S. Army scout, died in combat on the Allied front lines in Italy in 1944.

poet is sometimes capricious and [the] engineer uses his great talent to perform stunts. (Incidentally, he spent only one year at an engineering school; so his skill here is not the result of adequate technical preparation but rather the result of an imagination capable of thinking directly in terms of materials and constructive devices, instead of having to fulfill himself here through the offices of an assistant.) Nobody else has contributed such a range of fresh forms to architecture as Wright has done; and in every period of his development, even that since 1930, he has done superb single buildings that, to my mind, outshine the work of most of his contemporaries. Such, for example, is the Willey house in Minneapolis, which he finished around 1937 or 1938.[3]

But this great genius has equally great weaknesses: both his personality and his buildings show flaws that run from the top to the bottom of the structure. His greatest weakness is a monstrous ego: though he talks of democracy, he has the manners and beliefs of a Renascence prince: at heart he is a despot. His despotism is so all-embracing that he resents the very existence of his clients: he once reproved my friends the Hannas, at Palo Alto, after they had made a few trifling changes, adding a floor lamp and throwing a few llama rugs over their sofa, by saying: "You have spoiled this house completely: it is not a Frank Lloyd Wright house any longer, it is a Paul Hanna house!"[4] He deliberately designs low doorways, so that people over six feet high will bump their heads: he himself is a short man! In every room, no matter how private, he insists upon being visibly present: never for a moment shall you be permitted to forget the original architect himself.

But there is still another weakness, which one hardly perceives till one reviews the bulk of his work, as I did a few years ago at the Modern Museum show; and that is, he is, for all his ingenious surprises and innovations, a formalist: he begins with a preconceived idea, like that of a hexagon or a circle, and he carries it out in every detail, without regard to need or to function, precisely as the classic architect sacrificed his interiors ruthlessly to the need for balanced fenestration

---

3 Frank Lloyd Wright, Malcolm Willey House, Minneapolis, 1932–1934.

4 Paul Hanna (1902–1988), educator and client of Frank Lloyd Wright; Jean and Paul Hanna Residence, Palo Alto, 1935. Mumford and his family lived for a brief time in the Hanna Residence while he was a professor at Stanford University in the early 1940s.

on his facade. In the Hanna house, designed on a hexagonal pattern, every item of the furniture is askew; indeed , even the beds were designed askew and sheets had to be cut on a new pattern to cover them. The unity he thus achieves mechanically is an over-riding one; he is prepared to sacrifice far more important qualities to achieve it. I regard it as a serious flaw in architecture when the esthetic pattern becomes an obstacle to the integration of the whole. In too many instances, this happens in Wright's work. But every now and then he comes through with a building in which all the architectural elements, inner and outer, are worked into a complete whole; and when that happens, no one is his superior. Few architects in any age have had anything like his feeling for the site and the surrounding landscape: in that respect, he is the most universal of our architects in the very act of being the most regional.

One more point. Wright is a creator of individual buildings. Apart from the landscape, he has no sense of the whole. Hence his Broadacre City is a collection of individual buildings on single acre plots: in other words, not a city at all in any visible sense, even from the air. In every sense of the word, he is an isolationist. He and I broke in early 1941—or late in 1940—when he denounced people like myself, who urged American participation in the War, as gangsters: at that I wrote him a letter which completely terminated our relations on my side, though he himself occasionally favors me with Pecksniffian greetings, in which he expresses his charitable feelings toward those who will have none of him. But recently a young Italian named Bruno Zevi, who had interviewed Wright for a whole week, got him talking about me.[5] Wright denounced me bitterly. A little later they were discussing the possibility of a new architectural magazine and Zevi said to him: "You understand Mr. Wright, that there is only one possible editor for this kind of magazine?" To which Wright answered: "Of course: Lewis Mumford."

That little story shows the old rogue at his lovable best; arrogant, violent, despotic, high-handed, and yet with an occasional gleam of self-criticism or an occasional act of self-transcendence that redeems him. It is the character that he himself presents in his autobiography. In that book, he contributes data on his worst side that his enemies

5 Bruno Zevi (1918–2000), Italian writer, editor, and architectural historian.

might well think twice before using. Do you remember how he beat up the young Japanese in Sullivan's office?[6]

It is good to know, dear John, that your own great gifts are turned to the assessment of American culture: Mills College is to be congratulated on having the wisdom to invite you to give these lectures.[7] I plan to go to England in June, to lecture under the auspices of my old colleagues in the Institute of Sociology. When I come back I hope to finish my memoir of young Geddes and then start in good earnest on the last volume of my big series.[8] Sophia joins me in warm greetings to you and your wife

Ever yours
[signed]
Lewis

[ts&ms uarlf]

---

6 According to Wright's account in *An Autobiography* (p. 124), he assaulted—in his own Chicago office—a Japanese draftsman he had previously fired for inappropriate conduct around 1893.

7 Mills College, Oakland, California, where John Gould Fletcher lectured in summer 1946.

8 Lewis Mumford, *The Conduct of Life* (New York: Harcourt, Brace and Company, 1951). Volume 4 of The Renewal of Life.

1951

With the postwar economy in full swing, Wright and the Fellowship are busier than ever with a wide range of commissions, including the Solomon R. Guggenheim Museum in New York. Mumford, having finally completed The Renewal of Life, turns his attention to teaching and research. The correspondence is resumed at Wright's initiative around June 1951. At the risk of exacerbating old tensions, Mumford sends Wright a copy of *Green Memories*, an intimate biography of his son Geddes who was killed in the war. Once again, Wright invites the critic to visit him at Taliesin, but previous commitments and illnesses intervene.

[C. MAY—JUNE 1951]
[INSCRIPTION IN *The Sovereignty of the Individual*;
TRANSCRIBED IN LEWIS MUMFORD, *Sketches From Life*][1]

In spite of all—

your old F. Ll. W.

1 Frank Lloyd Wright, *The Sovereignty of the Individual: In the Cause of Architecture*, privately printed, 1951; reprint of preface to *Ausgeführte Bauten and Entwürfe von Frank Lloyd Wright*.

AMENIA, NEW YORK

28 JUNE 1951

Dear F.L.W.:

It was good of you to send me your Preface to the Berlin and Florence Exhibitions, as fresh and meaningful today as it was when it was originally written; and it was gracious of you to inscribe it as you did.[1] In the same spirit I am sending you a fragment of the book on *The Conduct of Life* that will be published in the fall, the final volume of my big series.[2] There is a chapter on Love in that book, as the only force capable of saving our loveless and death-seeking civilization—and it is high time, in our relations, that I exhibited a little of this quality myself, with all that goes with it. But you were in my mind and praise of your work and example was on my lips, in various public lectures, including the Bampton series I lately gave at Columbia, long before your preface came: so we have met, after all, half way, with the past forgotten and I hope, on both sides, forgiven.[3]

Much has happened since we last met: you have grown younger and I have grown older. My son Geddes, who was bred as a country boy, skilled in trapping and hunting, barely had the opportunity to demonstrate his resourcefulness and courage before he was killed in Italy, at the age of nineteen. (I wrote a little biography of him, which tells about the work and days of our family and neighbors as well; and if you have not come across it, I will be glad to send it to you. A handful of people think, and I with them, that it is the best thing I have written; but only a handful have read the book.)[4] We have a daughter of sixteen left, Alison, a girl of great spirit and promise, with a keen mind and great psychological penetration, too; and for her sake, because she needs the stimulus of a great city and can benefit even by

---

1 Wright, *The Sovereignty of the Individual*. This piece served as a preface to the exhibition, *Frank Lloyd Wright: Sixty Years of Living Architecture*, which opened in June 1951 at the Palazzo Strozzi, Florence after a previous showing in Philadelphia. It subsequently traveled to several European and American cities.

2 Lewis Mumford, *Man as Interpreter* (New York: Harcourt, Brace and Company, 1950).

3 Lewis Mumford, *Art and Technics* (New York: Columbia University Press, 1952). The Bampton Lectures in America, No. 4, Columbia University, New York.

4 Mumford, *Green Memories*.

its toughening, we have been living in New York in the winter, and shall live there one year more: after that we shall make this our permanent home once again.

The way in which you continue to flourish, like the Biblical bay tree, gives me immense pleasure; and though the honors that are now pouring into your lap are belated they at least give some measure of the mark you have left upon all of us. It is easy to conquer posterity: the hard job for an original mind is to make any dent on its contemporaries; and you have solved that problem by magnificently outliving those who could not take your measure because they were too near to you. As for me, with *The Conduct of Life* I finish the major work of the last twenty-one years of my life; and I must now make myself ready for the next phase, which will issue out of it and yet, I trust, go beyond it. You will recognize Emerson, of course, in the final title, which was also used by Croce.[5] I deliberately took it in order to emphasize the underlying affiliation, despite all differences in personality and philosophy, which you, dear FLW, were first to recognize. I had Emerson's *English Traits* with me when I went to England in 1946; and when the Lord Mayor of Manchester gave me a dinner I reminded the company that Emerson had spoken there, in the midst of another grave crisis, 99 years before, and had said: "England is no place for fainthearted men." That phrase is almost the opening sentence of my new book; applying, not to England, but the world.

When you come to New York again, let us meet. I find it sad that you have never seen me in this place, though not so sad, perhaps, as that I've never seen you in Taliesin.

Ever yours
[signed]
Lewis

[ts flwa]

5 Benedetto Croce (1866–1952), Italian philosopher.

Dear Lewis:

Your letter has weeded our garden and the flowers are showing as fresh and beautiful as after a spring rain. The weeds are gone. By the roots.

I've missed you Lewis. Your's is an Emersonian mind but on your own terms. What a man he was and how we need such-now! I've read your little book and, what?[1] A man you are. I shall never cease to be aware of the fact that I owe to you primal appreciation and support when it took real courage for you to render it. That I count as one of the real honors that have "fallen into my lap." As to the others, well only those similar (they are rare) have any effect. Italy is such and took us to the Italian heart. We have just returned. Zevi spoke warmly of you and regretted the break between us.[2] I assured him there was one no longer.

Now how soon can you—will you—bring your wife and daughter for a week with us here at Taliesin Mid-west?

We have a pleasant guest-house on the hill-garden ready for you. Why not motor out (or fly out) and do say when?

I want to see you and we want you to see how we work here. In addition to mine you would find a great welcome here—all around. When will you shake off the urban shackles and come to our country-home for a week?

(Send me the little memorial to the lost son.)

As ever, Affection
[signed]
Frank
Frank Lloyd Wright
July 10th, 1951

[pc ts&ms lmp]

1 Mumford, *Man as Interpreter*.
2 Bruno Zevi.

LEWIS MUMFORD
AMENIA, NEW YORK

3 AUGUST 1951

Dear Frank:

It was good to get your generous letter; and I'd have answered it sooner, if we had not spent ten days on the anxious seat, caused by an overzealous local doctor's advising Sophy to have an immediate operation. When we finally consulted a New York surgeon, just to be sure that it was urgent, he told Sophy to go home and forget about it entirely, dismissing her with the complete assurance of a man who really knows his business. Naturally, we are profoundly relieved, in fact exuberantly gay—though Sophy had been so persuaded by our nice country doctor that she had almost gone to the operating table on his say-so. But she still needs a long rest after an over-strenuous winter; and dearly though we'd both like to accept your invitation to Taliesin at once, Sophy is not up to any considerable amount of travelling; so that must wait. Meanwhile, the mere thought of it makes us, in anticipation, happy. As for me, this is my first bout of complete idleness in seven years, and I am enjoying it hugely. For the moment we are two very placid and contented animals, grazing in our garden and lazily watching the hours pass. This morning I will send off a copy of Green Memories. Here's to our meeting in a not-too distant-future....

Affectionately
[signed]
Lewis

[ts flwa]

Dear Lewis:

Glad Sophy went home. Chances are ten to one (always) against operation. She is actively strong—has a good mind and will get well—my wager.

I am sending you both a little memento of "the collection" (yes, it still exists).[1] A little more obvious than the sort of thing you are usually asked to see. But—refreshing just the same?

Affection, Come soon!
[signed]
Frank
Frank Lloyd Wright
August 6th, 1951

[pc ts&ms lmp]

1 *Kanda Temple in Snow*, a color woodblock print by Utagawa Hiroshige (1797–1858), which was part of a once extensive collection of Japanese prints owned by Wright.

[INSCRIPTION ON COLOR WOODBLOCK PRINT BY UTAGAWA HIROSHIGE, C. AUGUST 1951]

Kanda Temple in Snow Hiroshige
Yedo—Printed about 100 years ago—series "Tokyo Meisho"
Temple still exists

[signed]
F.LLW.

[ms Estate of Lewis and Sophia Mumford]

21 AUGUST 1951

Dear F.L.W.:

We've just come back from a fortnight by the sea, to find your beautiful gift waiting for us. That is a particularly fine Hiroshige, and it will have an honored place in our own modest collection. (My books, incidentally, are now coming out in a Japanese translation and I've been in close touch with my translator who lately visited us.)

Harcourt is sending you a copy of *The Conduct of Life*. Pay no attention to their request for a quotable sentence about it: your being on their "list" imposes no duties about me.

The nightmare of the unnecessary operation was washed out by the salt sea and we are all very happy.

With warmest thanks,

Ever yours,
[signed]
Lewis

[ms flwa]

Yes, Lewis, better than excellent criticism. If only the significance of architecture could be read by "supposedly living people" they would see Hitlerism Stalinism rampant in that costly crate in which to ship Freedom to its doom: hate required, fear taught, denunciation of neighbors a public virtue, etc., etc.[1]

Appreciation and affection,

Frank Lloyd Wright
September 14th, 1951

[cc ts flwa]

---

1 An oblique reference to Lewis Mumford's criticism of the United Nations Headquarters in New York. See Lewis Mumford, "The Sky Line: Magic with Mirrors—I," *New Yorker* 27 (15 September 1951): 84–93; and Lewis Mumford, "The Sky Line: Magic with Mirrors—II," *New Yorker* 27 (22 September 1951): 99–106.

1952

Mumford, who is editing an anthology of American architectural writings, asks Wright for permission to reprint three of his essays. Wright complies, but expresses his annoyance, specifically with a recent historical survey of the skyscraper, and more generally with historians and critics who are biased by the seemingly ubiquitous International Style. In February, Wright is scheduled to visit New York City in connection with the Guggenheim Museum project, and he and Mumford eagerly discuss their reunion. Conducted over lunch at the Plaza Hotel, their first meeting in more than a decade is a great success. Wright makes some rough architectural sketches of early works—from the time he worked in Sullivan's office—for Mumford to keep.

LEWIS MUMFORD
153 WEST 82ND STREET
NEW YORK 24. N.Y.

4 JANUARY 1952

Dear F.L.W.:

Happy New Year to you! I trust you and yours are flourishing.

This note is to ask you for permission to reprint your famous address on the Machine (in the Princeton Lectures) and your essays on Wyoming & Arizona in a book of readings I am getting out on the Modern Tradition in American Architecture.[1]

It will be a rich and varied book, from Thoreau & Greenough onward, and will, all in all, be worthy of your own contribution.[2]

Warmly
[signed]
Lewis

[ms flwa]

---

1 Frank Lloyd Wright, "The Art and Craft of the Machine," reprinted within Frank Lloyd Wright, "Machinery, Materials and Men," in *Modern Architecture*, 7–23; Frank Lloyd Wright, "The Bad Lands," letter to the editor, *The [Huron, South Dakota] Evening Huronite* (28 September 1935), reprinted in *Frank Lloyd Wright on Architecture: Selected Writings, 1894–1940*, edited with an introduction by Frederick Gutheim (New York: Duell, Sloan and Pearce, 1941), 191–196; Frank Lloyd Wright, "To Arizona," *Arizona Highways* 16 (May 1940): 8–13 and reprinted in *Frank Lloyd Wright on Architecture: Selected Writings*, 196–199. When making this request, Mumford seemed to have erred geographically. He ultimately reprinted only "The Art and Craft of the Machine"; see *Roots of Contemporary American Architecture: A Series of Thirty-Seven Essays Dating from the Mid-Nineteenth Century to the Present*, edited with an introduction by Lewis Mumford (New York: Reinhold Publishing Company, 1952), 169–185.
2 Horatio Greenough (1805–1852), American sculptor and writer.

Dear Lewis:

A letter to you has been there on my mind since the books so kindly sent by your publishers. Reading was delayed by an acute attack of bronchitis which deprived me of nearly every normal activity for many weeks. Together with knocking both Taliesins to pieces to substantiate them for the next century or so I have been left with only time to sleep. But now I am using myself again much as I please.

As you know, I like your work; find it honest and prophetic—both more rare qualities now than ever. The tribute to the boy I did not know (your boy) affected me deeply in your behalf.[1] But you know my feeling about the sacrifices demanded by war. I can't go along with any of it except in the realm of ideas. Even there I do not like to fight to kill but to save the human interests. So do you, I know. So let's forget what differences there are between us. I am sure they are not worth much.

The new work you propose is really for you. Only you could do it honestly with understanding. So it should be done by you now.

I've just received a book from the Chicago University Press on "The Rise of the Skyscraper" sodden with fact and false in spirit because there was an axe to grind: manifest to me, at least.[2] The publishers wanted me to write (for use as a blurb) what I thought of it..

I said, "acknowledging the research, I see the affair, from the inside, quite differently. It is apparently going to be hard for History to make an honest man of itself."

They didn't use it but put a blurb for "When Democracy Builds" on the back of the jacket.[3] You will scan the book of course. It is as far from the spirit of the whole thing as was Morrison's book on Sullivan.[4] I am beginning to feel that HISTORY—at best—is made by some man studying a profile seen from where he sits. At worst it is likely false. I have seen this "rise" and what came along with it for fifty-nine years of active work, in it and of it—Such history as I've read (by Gideon [*sic*], say) and from many pens is so specious a pretense of knowledge—that

1 Mumford, *Green Memories*.
2 Carl W. Condit, *The Rise of the Skyscraper* (Chicago: University of Chicago Press, 1952).
3 Frank Lloyd Wright, *When Democracy Builds* (Chicago: University of Chicago Press, [1945]).
4 Hugh Morrison, *Louis Sullivan: Prophet of Modern Architecture* (New York: Norton, 1935).

my gorge rises as I read.[5] The whole affair is overlaid with this, that, and the other "effect" without due reference to cause or truth until the whole business looks to the reader as would an indiscriminate washout on the line. Whose shirt—whose pants—belonged to whom? The historian doesn't really know so tags them for himself, as he sits to view the wash.

History? A post-mortem. Of course. But does it need be according to some personal bias? Or edited to sell the book? What is "Editorial policy" in our country but salesmanship? What will sell the paper, magazine or book. Even the crusading editor is dead and in his place reigns "the Big-Interest."

So if your work is honest it will only sell to the now young generation. The one to which we belong will resent it. The one after ours will find itself exposed and turn away. The present operators, big and small, don't give a damn so long as they can cash in.

The truth of the whole affair is so encrusted with Bauhaus, Museum of Modern Art, Hitchcock and Johnson, provincial imports of culture from abroad and commercialization of the original ideas that any post mortem held by anyone (except one in the know by experience like yourself) is phony or bogus.

The Bandwagon is filled to overflowing and is being stalled by its own freight of "also-rans" in the commercial gutter. The "plan-factory" is their gutter.

Anyway, Lewis, you must come—before long—to Taliesin West. We want to see you and Sophie here this very winter for a week or two. How can I help you arrange this and when?

I am to be in New York (on the Guggenheim) February 4th.[6] Will stay at the Plaza and I hope we can arrange the visit to the desert then.[7] Why couldn't I bring you both back with me?

---

5 Sigfried Giedion, *Space, Time and Architecture: The Growth of a New Tradition* (Cambridge, Massachusetts: Harvard University Press, 1941); Sigfried Giedion (1888–1968), Swiss architectural historian, writer, and critic.

6 Frank Lloyd Wright, Solomon R. Guggenheim Museum, New York, 1943–1959.

7 Wright traditionally stayed at the Plaza Hotel when in New York. In 1954, while at work on the Guggenheim Museum, he remodeled a suite at the Plaza to serve as his New York office and residence.

Affection,
[signed]
F.LL.W.
Frank Lloyd Wright
January 10, 1952

N.B. Help yourself to anything I have that you want. Zevi is undertaking the big collection of my work (in color) in Italy. You like him. He likes you. [signed] FLLW.

[pc ts&ms lmp]

21 JANUARY 1952

Dear F.L.W.:

It was good to hear from you and it will be even better to see you when you are here on the fourth. I trust your damned bronchitis is now completely vanished: the healthier one is fundamentally the more disgusting these attacks are, as I well know. Thank you for your generous invitations and permissions. The last I take gladly: but the first alas! I can't, because of a succession of engagements, accept.

With all eagerness,

Ever yours
[signed]
Lewis

[ms flwa]

[C. JANUARY 1952]

My dear Lewis:

Refusing my earnest invitation to come help Taliesin fills me with a vague fear—a fear that I shall, never again, meet the Llewis [*sic*] I loved—he who lived and wrote out of love and understanding, let fall what might—my valiant, vibrant, independently honest Llewis—the Mumford.[1]

I now see you have been more badly hurt than I supposed and that therefore I may meet a broadened but wisened [*sic*] professionalized writer with the ifs, buts and alsos of his craft, temporizing for fame, himself a slave of livelihood? I fear because my Llewis, no matter what, would not plead "engagement" when asked with love to this capitol of the modern world of Architecture to share experience with love and understanding of this work he was once bound to cherish. (Yes, I refer to this little America within America we call Taliesin)—a radical work he has never seen, where he would naturally feel and be at home with what he loved as his own.

And Llewis—how richly well Taliesin could afford to transport you and your Sophie to this Architecture of the Valley of the Sun—plant you both in a little cottage here (your own for a fortnight or as you liked—and would—) and asking only that you talk to the boys at Sunday morning breakfast and let them talk to you and you answer their queries again Sunday evening. There are 60 of them from all over the world.

If you drive yourself you would have an M.G. to wander about wild Arizona. Or if you don't drive—a Chrysler and driver to take you. Between times, as the spirit moved, we could talk or not talk as we used to do. And then we would send you back by way of Frisco, if you wanted to go that way, to experience the Morris shop etc, etc.[2] Your "Bay-region" you know![3]

You have never seen the work of these later years.

Well—here you see the arrogance you find in me because I suppose you could have no "engagement" that could matter enough to hold

1 A Welsh-inspired variant of Lewis.

2 Frank Lloyd Wright, V. C. Morris Gift Shop, San Francisco, 1948.

3 A reference to the Bay Region style of northern California, which Mumford embraced as but one of many regional alternatives to the International Style. See Lewis Mumford, "The Sky Line: Status Quo," *New Yorker* 23 (11 October 1947): 104–106.

you away from that experience in the circumstances, I propose. You see, Llewis being so sure of my ground and my star so early in life, I was soon forced to choose between honest arrogance and a hypocritical humility.

Well, the world knows I chose honest arrogance. Nor am I sorry. Nor is my Cause. You didn't used to mind? You do mind now, because—well—you have so said.

And so, I fear, that he—the Llewis of my youth may be no more. Suddenly I am afraid I shall find in his place the professionialized successful Critic with unbreakable engagements—an E. M. Forster "Critic" (see his last book "Two Cheers for Democracy" and read his piece on the "Raison d'etre of Criticism," if you have not already read it).[4] You will see there what I mean.

No, you have never really experienced the creative work into which the work of those early years has developed. I don't think a man like you needs drink a tub of dye to know what color it is—but—because there was love and understanding between us that is why the rupture was so violent. Whatever the Llewis may now be that I am to meet in New York about the first of February, though the same old depth may no longer apply, yet there may be something precious to preserve?

At any rate, like a man hungry for the honesty of the romantic understanding that is courageous love, I shall be grateful and pleasant as I know you will be for whatever may be left to me.

Llewis—"engagements" in such circumstances as I propose are a cruel bond? Are we too old to break them to play hookey once more?

Arrogant as ever—you see?—with the same old affection and new nostalgia.

[signed]
Frank
Frank Ll. . . .

NB By the way, do you reprove me for the ancestral double L by never using it yourself?

[signed]
FLlW

[pc ts&ms lmp, c. January 1952]

4 E. M. Forster, *Two Cheers for Democracy* (New York: Harcourt, Brace and Company, 1951); E. M. Forster, "Raison d'etre of Criticism," *Horizon* 18 (December 1948): 397–411.

LEWIS MUMFORD
153 WEST 82 STREET
NEW YORK 24. N.Y.

TR3-7783

2 FEBRUARY 1952

Dear F. Ll. W.:

Welcome to New York! Will you and your wife have lunch or dinner with us—or shall we come to you? We'd both delight to have you here—not in our house but our winter camp!

How did my wretched hand betray me with Llyod[*sic*]—there! You see it's still betraying me, for some deep psychological reason, no doubt—though in the typewriter I never fail you! It's as bad as people calling me Louis. Forgive me!

As for my having changed—it's rather the contrary that keeps me from cancelling long-made lecture engagements to go off to you this winter. The pattern is an old one, alas! And I have already lived to regret it.

But it's a dozen years since we met & much has happened: so don't be too shocked.

Affectionately
[signed]
Lewis

[ms flwa]

[INSCRIPTION IN UNIDENTIFIED HAND ON SKETCH BY FRANK LLOYD WRIGHT]

FLW—In England—
Aristocracy hasn't
earned privileges.
In America we have
conferred privileges
on unprivileged[.]
Result is far worse.

7 Feb. 1952 [IN HAND OF LEWIS MUMFORD]

[pc lmp]

Dear Llewis:—!sic!

I can't tell you how good it was to be with you again in spirit as well as bodily presence which is essentially the same vital Llewis. The amazing comprehension, as of the earlier days of our friendship, is still vibrant. You were never so much the critic as the creative writer, champion of cultural causes—Llewis. Little good our journalistic sort of critics do our Causes. Even less harm they do to evil ones than good to noble ones because radio, press, and print crawl with them like flies on a window pane.

So goes everything we have—prolix but not prolific. We are getting too enormous for a Democracy. Unless we create for ourselves our own eddy in some swirl of the backwater we are washed out and away with the current into internationalism and the commonplace.

• • • • • • •

Funny thing happened. Got home with a commission from a New York magazine to write 2000 words for $1000.00 on any subject I chose and had it well along when a letter came from the *Record*'s editor asking me to write something for the *Record* myself, since I was continually referred to on its pages. Offered me $500.00 for the job. Remembering with gratitude, still, old Dr. Mikklesen's calling me in (when I was getting a worm's eye view of society in New York, 1927) to suggest that I write seven articles for the *Record* for which he would pay $7,500.00 (that was money then).[1] "Choose my own subject." I wrote "The Nature of Materials." There was nothing on the subject in literature so I found when I wanted to study the subject. This is in retrospect. Cheerful. I can afford the loss and be happy.

So I have two loyalties to publishers—one to Howard Myers; one to Dr. Mikkelsen.[2] Both editors are now dead and I guess the magazines are not far from it? Except for advertising.

Copy of the article is herewith.[3] If you care to read it. Gene made only one so kindly return at your convenience.[4]

---

1 H. H. Mikklesen, editor of *Architectural Record*. See Wright's series for the *Record*, "In the Cause of Architecture" (1927–1928), cited above.

2 Howard Myers (d. 1947), editor of *Architectural Forum*, responsible for Wright's two monograph issues in January 1938 and January 1948.

3 Frank Lloyd Wright, "Organic Architecture Looks at Modern Architecture," *Architectural Record* 111 (May 1952): 148–154.

My best to you and your handsome Sophie. We'll have dinner (all four) together next March on our way to Paris—say about the 29th. I hope. The show opens at the Paris Beaux Arts, April 3rd.[5]

Affection as ever,
[signed]
F.Ll.W., Frank!
Frank Lloyd Wright
February 20th, 1952

[ts jscl]

---

4 Eugene Masselink.
5 *Frank Lloyd Wright: Sixty Years of Living Architecture*.

LEWIS MUMFORD
153 WEST 82 STREET
NEW YORK 24, N.Y.

27 FEBRUARY 1952

Dear F. LL.W.:

You beat me to the draw, or rather, to the letterbox; but I have gone around for weeks now with a happy smile on my face, in recollection of our meeting and of the happy solidarity and understanding and sweetness that attended it. When there is bedrock beneath a relationship it doesn't matter how much debris may, by accident, pile on top of it, or how many differences there may be in the superficial levels that show themselves above it. You and I both know certain differences remain and will always remain, between us; but since neither of us is afraid of differences as such—unlike the people who are trying to regiment our country into a compulsive uniformity—we can take all that in our stride. It was good to see you: good to hear you: good to clasp your hand again: good to see Olgivanna, magnificent even when she is ill or in pain. And since there is a sense in which re-union gives one a keener consciousness of what joins people than the union one sometimes takes for granted, I might almost bless the breach that brought us together again, if that didn't make me sound like an unctuous Baptist! . . . Thank you for letting me see your magnificent diatribe on the "modern."[1] I'm returning it under separate cover. The book of essays I have been gathering together will back you up further, by showing how deep in our bones the organic was and is, and how superficial the post-1920 modern was.[2] As for the UN building, it was cast in the image of automatism and bureaucracy, and it is those twin agents, the mechanical function and the mechanical functionary, both divorced from the subordinate position they might occupy in the interests of life, that constitute the real menace of our time, it seems to me. I am not afraid of internationalism. If our own roots are deep, so that we can absorb outside influences and make them our own, as they can absorb our influences in the same wise, we shall all be the better for

1 Wright, "Organic Architecture Looks at Modern Architecture."
2 Mumford, ed., *Roots of Contemporary American Architecture*.

the mixings and cross-fertilizations that are taking place now and will do so even more fully in future. That building is a perfect image, of course, of our topsy turvy world in which the machine takes over the functions of the person and reduces him to a nullity.

. . . How well I remember that episode with the *Architectural Record*: for this happened the year I first met you—indeed it was on that very visit that we came together. I also remember my excitement over the articles when they came out; and I wonder now why you didn't publish them as a book. There is nothing like them in literature; and the extracts that Gutheim published in his book are not sufficiently full to serve instead of the complete articles.[3] Why don't you take this up with your publishers? I'm sure they'd be eager to do such a book. But how everything has gone down hill, as regards the value set on writing—as indicated by what editors will pay for it. When Goble offered me twice as much for an article as the *Record* had paid in 1929, I told him that at corrected prices I was barely holding my own; and that he was making no allowance for the fact that my value should have increased in twenty years![4]

We are eager to see you and Olgivanna when you come through on the twenty-ninth. I shall keep the calendar clear. With affectionate greetings to you both

[signed]
Lewis

[ts&ms flwa]

3 Gutheim, ed., *Frank Lloyd Wright on Architecture*.

4 Emerson Goble (1901–1969), managing editor of *Architectural Record*.

[WITH PHOTOGRAPHIC ENCLOSURE]

Dear F.L.W.:

This is my "country face"—the one you've never alas! seen on its native soil, as indeed I've never seen yours yet on your land. But it's through the soil, isn't it? that our roots come together. . . .

[signed]
Lewis
26 April 1952

[ms flwa]

SUNDAY
27 APRIL 1952

. . . Strange, dear Frank: I sealed the envelope with this picture yesterday: and this morning I read, with dismay, of your loss—our loss—of the Hillside School.[1] But I know how you turn losses into opportunities. . . .

[signed]
Lewis

[ms flwa]

1 The Hillside Home School building was badly damaged by a fire and subsequently rebuilt.

HARKNESS PAVILION[1]
180 FORT WASHINGTON AVENUE
NEW YORK 32. N.Y.

14 AUGUST 1952

Dear Frank and Olgivanna:

Unless rumor has told you otherwise you probably still think I am kiting around Europe. But the fact is that I came down at the beginning of May with an attack of dysentery (picked up in Raleigh!) which produced complications: and that in turn disclosed a danger from an oversized prostate, which might at any time or place, repeat the same dangerous performance of closing up the bladder.[2] After trying a month of "treatments" it became plain that an operation was inevitable: so here I am, with the operation thirteen days behind me, feeling fit as the proverbial fiddle. Sophy & I had three beautiful tranquil weeks in the country before coming down here: so I faced the "ordeal" in a state of yoga-like detachment, and enjoyed almost every moment of it, because of the inner peace and quiet my state carried with it.

I hope you both are well and happy. On Monday we go back to Amenia—I, physically sterilized but spiritually fertile!

Affectionately
[signed]
Lewis

[ms flwa]

1 Columbia-Presbyterian Medical Center, New York.
2 Mumford was a visiting professor at North Carolina State College in Raleigh between 1948 and 1952.

My dear Lewis:

Often thinking of you as happy in Italy this summer, returning from Mexico we were shocked to learn that you were all the time at a hospital in New York. Thank God that is over. We are happy to learn that you are now at Amenia chastened, but not resentful, cleaned up and recovering.

At least you are all together there in a place you love and have made home—"Home Is Best" is a motto I used to "work" in colored worsted on perforated cardboard in my Boston kindergarten days.[1] I now know the old saws are, at least, true.

We would love to have you all in our guest house here at Taliesin for September or October or any part of either should the spirit move you to come.

Our love to you and your Sophie, including the lovely young Mumford. She might like lively Iovanna.[2]

Affection and Faith—
[signed]
Frank and Olgivanna
August 30th, 1952

[pc ts&ms lmp]

1 A reference to Friedrich Froebel's Kindergarten method taught to Wright by his mother.

2 Iovanna Lloyd Wright (b. 1925), daughter of Frank Lloyd Wright and Olgivanna Lloyd Wright.

Dear Lewis:

You are often the subject of our conversation, have a deep place in our hearts and are the object of our solicitude. How is the "come back" now?

Are you out of it all and back on the top where you belong again?

Just a note to let us know.

We will be in New York at the usual place (the Plaza) about the eighth of November.

Affection,
Frank Lloyd Wright
October 15th, 1952

[cc ts flwa]

LEWIS MUMFORD
AMENIA, NEW YORK

19 OCTOBER 1952

Dear Frank:

It was good to get your first letter back in September and even better to get your second—which by happy chance came in time for my birthday! (Today) You'd have heard from me sooner but for the fact that my three courses at the Univ. of Pennsylvania absorbed all my energy—more at first than I had to give.[1] I look as healthy and big as an old-fashioned brewer, and am in fact completely healed and whole. But the body remembers the violence done to it, it seems, and begrudges energy for any other tasks but its own. Still, I improve daily & people who have been through serious operations say this is all commonplace.

I shall be in Boston the weekend you are coming to New York; but I'll try to get hold of you coming through on my way back to Phila. (My address is The Drake, Phila. 2)

With affectionate greetings to you both
[signed]
Lewis

[ms flwa]

1 Mumford was a visiting professor at the University of Pennsylvania in Philadelphia between 1951 and 1956, and 1959 and 1961.

1953

Mumford's anthology, *Roots of Contemporary American Architecture*, has been published with Wright's revised essay "The Art and Craft of the Machine" included. The oft-discussed topics of the International Style and the influence of Hitchcock and Johnson are revisited. Wright praises Mumford's somewhat harsh assessment of the United Nations complex for the *New Yorker*. Mumford in turn reflects on his role as an architecture critic.

A retrospective exhibition of Wright's work, *Sixty Years of Living Architecture*, opens in a temporary pavilion on the site of the future Guggenheim Museum in November. After viewing it with Wright as his guide, Mumford writes a two-part review of the show for the *New Yorker* that also examines unsparingly the larger tableau of the architect's life and work.

Dear Llewis: ? like Lloyd—

Long time since we have seen or heard from the Mumfords. I have an uneasy feeling that sickness may again, be the cause. But, I hope not.

I am sure the holidays brought to you and yours what you richly deserve—happiness. We have not been too well ourselves which may, after all, be the basis of our fears for you.

The desert this year is especially alluring. You all ought to see it. The place we live in here would be a good place for you to come to when the spirit moves you. There is so much to tell and talk about since we last met. But we are so completely detached that we not only see nothing of you but hear nothing about you. I am taking the liberty of sending you a pressing of the record made of the talk I gave the Junior A. I. A. last fall.[1] The records are a new phase of our enterprize. There is now quite a gallery of them but this one I think would be of especial interest to you.

Let me know something of your plans and activities for the near future so we may arrange meeting if possible?

Our love to Sophie and the lovely young Mumford. Be assured of our affection and best hope for you all,

[signed]
Frank
Frank Lloyd Wright
January 5th, 1953

[pc ts lmp]

1 Frank Lloyd Wright, "Talk Given to the Junior American Institute of Architects of New York City," Waldorf-Astoria Hotel, New York, private pressing, Columbia Records, July 1952.

THE DRAKE
SPRUCE STREET-WEST OF FIFTEENTH
PHILADELPHIA 2

10 JANUARY 1953

... How good it was to get your letter, dear Frank; and how keen your intuitions were about the state of things with me. Our holidays were happy because we were together again, all three of us, in our beloved old farmhouse which fits us like an old glove and is just as shabby as a doll that has been too long fondled. But during this very vacation I found myself distracted by an abscessed tooth—which had a considerable time before, apparently, become devitalized. It was this, and not the after-effects of my operation, that had made me feel dull, depressed, sleepy, and averse to any sort of real work all fall. But the operation had thrown both me and the doctor off the scent, though I should have remembered a similar occasion twenty years before. All the plans I had made for the coming spring, including my so-long-deferred plan of visiting with you, have now been ruined; for the tooth is a front tooth, unfortunately, and its removal will involve a long and tedious bit of reconstruction. Forgive this over-detailed and lugubrious response to your fine greeting. I am much more concerned with the fact that you and Olgivanna have not been so well; and I trust that the early spring that comes to the desert will quickly revive you both. My time will be spent this spring, I suspect, shuttling back and forth between Amenia and New York for my dental work, trying in the meanwhile to sandwich in some of the writing I had planned to do before going to Europe in May.

I wonder if the book I edited on *The Roots of Contemporary American Architecture* ever caught up with you: chiefly, perhaps, I wonder because I hope you liked the little biography of you I wrote for it, and approved of my selections from your work.[1] If it got lost at one or another of the Taliesins I'll have the publisher send you another copy. Our daughter Alison has been having a very exciting time at college, for she has some very penetrating and stimulating professors and

1 "Frank Lloyd Wright (1869–)" in *Roots of Contemporary American Architecture*, 435–436.

she is full of delight at watching her own mind unfold, as a morning glory does when the sun rises. Her intuitions are often surer than her knowledge, and she reaches out to embrace in anticipation ideas she is not yet mature enough to handle. In all she gives us great hope—and constant delight.

We look forward to listening to your voice on the record you sent us, it will be waiting for us at Amenia when we go back there the last week in January—if we can keep to our present plans. Sophy joins me in embracing you both warmly.

Affectionately
[signed]
Lewis

[ts flwa]

Dear Lewis:

So sorry! but clouds will hang between us and the sun? We know they pass, and come again, but we go on. Forever. . . .

No,—I've seen no book. Do send me one. I shall value what you write. <u>You</u> have seen it all come in.

Give my love to the Amenia household—someday perhaps we will see you. We could so well afford to send you three return-trip plane tickets to get you here with our boys for a few days or as long as you cared to stay. Might that not be a good break for your health—here in the sun?

Affection,
[signed]
Frank
Frank Lloyd Wright
January 12th, 1953.

[pc ts&ms lmp]

LEWIS MUMFORD: AMENIA: NEW YORK

28 FEBRUARY 1953

. . . Thank you, dear Frank, for your generous invitation and your consolatory messages. Because there is little prospect this spring that I can accept the first, the second were all the more welcome. My dentist, poor man, came down with virus pneumonia; and this has left me more or less up in the air, with the tedious job of reconstruction still ahead of me. As a result of this delay I was able to give one more talk, at a centennial celebration of the Cooper Union: so full of challenging thoughts about the fear and suspicion and poisonous hatred and irrationality now rampant among our countrymen that not a word of it got into the newspapers. There is a sort of cold censorship at work that confirms and supports the mistakes of the cold war and the congealed minds that have been waging it. I haven't had a chance to more than glance at *Built in U.S.A.* yet, but I can imagine how infuriating it must be to you to find yourself alongside some of the people represented there.[1] Hitchcock is well meaning, but fundamentally insensitive to what goes on in a real work of architecture, though capable of being very learned, in an abstract way, about what he can get out of documents and books: so that it was right that he should have put the data about your own work in order, with the kind of thoroughness and persistence that work needs. But his usefulness stops there: Johnson, on the other hand, is ill-meaning and insidious: still the same man that admired Huey Long and the Nazis, though he now covers that up by voluble professions of democracy. . . . This spring, if my dentist grants me enough free time, I hope to write a little book on Love and Marriage that has long been pleasantly plaguing me: part of it was a chapter in *The Conduct of Life*, which I threw away.

Affectionate greetings from us both to you and Olgivanna

[signed]
Lewis

[ts&ms flwa]

---

1 *Built in U.S.A.: Postwar Architecture*, exhibition, Museum of Modern Art, New York, 20 January 1953 to 15 March 1953.

Dear Lewis:

Apropos all this "new" criticism—the "come back" was a come back only because the critics in my own country were obsessed by the Bau-haus and mistook that conversion for a revelation. You were the only one not so fooled.

But we did not hear from you at the proper moment.

How are you, Lewis.

Affection,
Frank Lloyd Wright
March 18th, 1953

[cc ts flwa]

To Lewis—(the Mumford)

. . . Better than ever! Your "Skyline"—U.N. Assembly—conclusion (last lines) is prophetic criticism for which you will be remembered.[1] The courageous conviction I admired in you from the first.

Vive the *New Yorker*! What other magazine would have dared? But the court-jester always spoke what other courtiers never dared utter.

Emerson would put his hand on your shoulder and say "my son"?

Affection,
[signed]
Frank
Frank Lloyd Wright
March 21st, 1953

[pc ts&ms lmp]

1 Lewis Mumford, "The Sky Line: United Nations Assembly," *New Yorker* 29 (14 March 1953): 72–81.

LEWIS MUMFORD: AMENIA: NEW YORK

26 MARCH 1953

. . . Your notes, dear Frank, have been better than any spring tonic. Praise never comes too often, and praise that one respects comes mighty seldom: so your word about my Sky Line on the UN touched me deeply indeed. There have been times when I rebelled against the work I did for *The New Yorker*: usually times when the subject matter itself was too trivial to be worth the time one had to spend upon it. But there are so few places left where it is possible to speak in a clean, straightforward fashion, with no regard for anything but clarity and truth, that I find myself holding on to the job as a sort of public duty. As for all the fallacies and pretenses of contemporary architectural criticism, dear Frank, I am tempted to say to you: Don't let them take five minutes away from your own creative work. In the long run those errors will be self-refuting, and if they are not, well, leave them to me to battle with, and to the young people who will be coming after both of us! Every new work of yours is a refutation.

This spring has been a queer, interrupted period for me; but one of the interruptions worked out to my benefit. My dentist came down with virus pneumonia and was out of commission for a month. When he came back, he had in the meanwhile come across the report of a new antibiotic that had been used successfully on my kind of infection. Now he is applying it at weekly intervals to my tooth; and there is some chance, a good one he thinks, that I may be spared for a few years the wholesale reconstruction that would otherwise be necessary.

Sophy and I, meanwhile, have had an idyllic two months here, watching the coming of spring from the first tremor of red on the maples to the snowdrops, the winter aconite, and the scylla. It's the first winter since 1941 that we've spanned the whole range of changes. We trust you and Olgivanna have been having an equivalent joy in the desert.

Affectionately
[signed]
Lewis

[ts&ms flwa]

[INSCRIPTION IN "IN THE CAUSE OF ARCHITECTURE: THE 'INTERNATIONAL STYLE.'"][1]

To Llewis—
The battle is "joined"—

[signed]
Frank—
Taliesin West—April 20
53

[pc ms lmp]

1 Frank Lloyd Wright, "In the Cause of Architecture: The 'International Style,'" privately printed, Taliesin, February 1953.

LEWIS MUMFORD
AMENIA, NEW YORK

4 MAY 1953

Dear Frank:

This has been a broken spring for us from one end to another: the latest was a three week illness of Sophy's. But I am at last sailing for Europe day after tomorrow and I don't want to go without at least thanking you affectionately for many things—your recorded talk, your handsome photograph, your essays—and most of all for the impulse that prompted you to send them. I look forward to seeing you in the fall. Meanwhile, all blessings on you both.

Affectionately,
[signed]
Lewis

P.S. Sophy and Alison will follow me in June.

[ms flwa]

Dear Lewis:

By this time I hope you have had the wretched teeth out and away and no more anguish from that source. What you say of the twins at the Bauhaus gallery is just right.[1] To keep in touch, herewith the latest.[2]

Also a copy of an Italian appraisal.[3] Why couldn't Whiskers have written something like that.[4] Because he is not a Grancarlo de Carlos [*sic*], I guess.[5]

Best to Sophie and the lovely daughter.

Affection,
Frank Lloyd Wright
September 12
1953

N.B. If you are going to write on Love and Marriage, glance at the translation of Ellen Key on the subject.[6] Done by Mamah Bouton Borthwick while at Taliesin.[7] She lost her life there soon after she finished the work.

[cc ts flwa]

1 Henry-Russell Hitchcock, Jr. and Philip Johnson.

2 Probably Frank Lloyd Wright, "Excerpts from the 'International Style,'" *Architectural Record* 113 (June 1953): 12, 332.

3 Giancarlo de Carlo, "Wright and Europe," offprint of translation by Giovanni del Drago of "Wright e l'Europa," *Sele Arte* 1 (September–October 1952): 17–24.

4 Nickname for Henry-Russell Hitchcock, Jr.

5 Giancarlo de Carlo (b. 1919), Italian architectural critic.

6 Ellen Key, *The Morality of Women and Other Essays*, translated from the Swedish by Namah Bouton Bothwick [*sic*] (Chicago: Ralph Fletcher Seymour Co., 1911).

7 Mamah Bouton Borthwick (1869–1914), American writer and romantic companion of Frank Lloyd Wright.

[INSCRIPTION AT TOP OF "WRIGHT AND EUROPE" BY GIANCARLO DE CARLO]

Lewis,

This had to be said by Europe—nobody home to tell the truth—?

[signed]
Frank

[pc ms lmp]

LEWIS MUMFORD
AMENIA, NEW YORK

26 OCTOBER 1953

Dear Frank;

I've been trying for a whole month to get around to telling you how pleased I was to hear your welcoming voice on the phone, even though it found us in the trying confusion of unpacking and repacking. And now your note comes to us, while up here on our last weekend before closing up the house for the autumn, with the pleasant news that you, as well as your exhibition, will be open to inspection next week.[1] As a matter of fact, we hope to be in the city late in the afternoon of Thursday, the twenty second; and could see you any time that day from five on, or any time on Friday up to five o'clock in the afternoon. I hope that, one day or the other, you can wedge in a few minutes for us in your busy life. I am eager to traverse your Sixty Years of high achievement; so, whether in flesh or in spirit or both, we'll meet soon.

With affectionate greetings from us both to you and Olgivanna,

Ever yours
[signed]
Lewis

P.S. I'm teaching again at The University of Pennsylvania; and live in The Drake, Phila. 2.

[ts & ms flwa]

1 Letter unlocated; *Frank Lloyd Wright: Sixty Years of Living Architecture*, exhibition, New York, November 1953.

THE DRAKE
PHILADELPHIA 2

23 NOVEMBER 1953

Dear Frank:

Yesterday I finished one of the most difficult tasks I have ever attempted: a criticism of your life & work in architecture. The first article will appear in The New Yorker this week: the second will come out the following issue, probably.[1] If I had wanted only to write an encomium that would have been easy; but it seemed to me that the moment demanded something more comprehensive, more penetrating, more judicious than this; and so, in fear and trembling and admiration and love I dared write the article about your work that no one else, friendly or hostile, has yet dared to write. I felt I owed it as a duty to you as well as to the coming generation; if I could not say all I felt needed to be said without disclosing real differences between us I still count upon the underlying solidities of our friendship to absorb the occasional shock. As usual "the best remains unsaid"; but you will find more than a hint of it in every paragraph.

In old friendship,
[signed]
Lewis

[ms flwa]

1 Lewis Mumford, "The Sky Line: A Phoenix Too Infrequent," *New Yorker* 29 (28 November 1953): 133–139; and Lewis Mumford, "The Sky Line: A Phoenix Too Infrequent—II," *New Yorker* 29 (12 December 1953): 116–127.

[TELEGRAM]

PA 590 LA 069
L.PFA 158 DL PD=PHOENIX ARIZ 29 1145 A MM= 1953 NOV
29 PM 2 41

LEWIS MUMFORD=
DRAKE HOTEL PHILA=

DEAR LEWIS:
THOUGH I HAVE NOT SEEN THE ARTICLE I AM GLAD[.]
YOU ARE THE ONLY ONE REALLY QUALIFIED TO CRITISIZE STOP IT IS THE PSYCHOLOGICAL MOMENT AND
WILL PROBABLY BE USED AS MY EPITAPH[.]

AFFECTION=

FRANK LLOYD WRIGHT=

[pc lmp]

[C. NOVEMBER–DECEMBER, 1953]

THE PLAZA
FIFTH AVENUE AT 59TH STREET
NEW YORK

Dear Lewis—

Read your "appreciation" in the plane coming in last night—both glad and furious—[1]

Read? Insults my clients and myself—I may be vain but I am not stupid—neither are my clients.

He harks back to the view that an individual should go to "a style" for his home, be the guest of a style rather than the guest of a great architect—? Yes?

Good argument for the communist against Democracy.

He should talk to my clients. So you talked to one—one Paul Hanna. From him you got a false impression—at least so he says and so say I.

Just one word slipped[;] the word "my" was actually "your" in reproving him for mixing his metaphors in living. As reprehensible as mixing them in writing. Your house said I—My house said you.

Well, I see the misquotations in the *New Yorker* article—in effect—

Now Lewis do you advocate that a man should shun the master and take the slave in order that his own individuality may not suffer eclipse.

If so, viva "Le International"—The communist wins over the Democrat? No, you don't mean that—you mean that the master is so vain in the power of his works that he sacrifices his client on the altar of his virtuosity.

The answer to that is from the clients themselves.

They will be heard from because your imputation via Sir Herbert Read will make them all boiling mad.[2] It is an unjust insult to their intelligence—(and mine).

But love to you just the same. You will learn better now—

Affection no end
[signed]
Frank

[pc ms lmp]

1 Mumford, "The Sky Line: A Phoenix Too Infrequent."
2 Sir Herbert Read (1893–1968), English poet and critic.

THE DRAKE
SPRUCE STREET-WEST OF FIFTEENTH
PHILADELPHIA 2

3 DECEMBER 1953

Dear Frank:

I grieve that you have taken my *New Yorker* criticism so ill; for the best praise of a man's work is not that which is unqualified, but that which remains after all qualifications. Once you have gotten over the shock of this report—in which I have dealt with your own life and work in the same loving but unsparing fashion I did with my own son's—I trust that you will be comforted by my writing, as perhaps the highest critical accolade that you have yet received. I wrote the second part of it two weeks ago, and finished revising the page proofs before your letter came; it will appear next week. Though it is in a sense an answer to your letter, it is an answer that anticipated it, by bringing out the essential differences between our respective philosophies of life. If the criticism of the second article strikes deeper and is even more painful, the praise, by the same token, rises higher. But on one matter I must set you right, if only to affirm Paul's unwavering loyalty to you. My judgement of your work has not been unduly affected by anything the Hannas said to me, or by the fact that the Hanna house is the only house of yours I have lived in: it is based on the reports of other clients than Paul, and above all, on the evidence of your buildings themselves. What you say there is more unmistakable than any conversations, or even than your own well-considered words. With deep respect and warm love still, as from one Master to another—

[signed]
Lewis

[ts flwa]

[C. DECEMBER 1953]

Dear Lewis:

I love you just the same. Ill? Don't get me wrong. I shall take my chastisement with my glory and few drops of blood on my forehead shall not mar the integrity of my love for the boy who wrote *Sticks and Stones*. He is one with me at the center of things.

What a misfortune that you should have lived in one of the several houses where the house outran the client by too far. I was engrossed with the idea that the hexagon is more suited to human habitation (owing to easier circulation) than the habitual rectangle that accommodated the carpenter, and Paul's intellectuality fooled both Paul and me.

There are so many houses well conceived as proper homes for those who own them—let's say 90%. The Lloyd Lewis for a perfect example.[1] Etc., Etc. Yes, Etc.

But the way of advance in a home as a true—(innate)—work of Art is not smooth, as a matter of course, and regret, as you must see. I am committed to it, however, and so are you whether you know it or not. And so is Sophie and so will Allison [*sic*] be. Our love to you all from where you should come see.

Affection,
[signed]
Frank
Frank Lloyd Wright

N. B. But even the Hanna House was merciful compared to The Farnsworth![2]

F. Ll. W.

[pc ts&ms lmp]

1 Lloyd Lewis residence, Libertyville, Illinois, 1939.

2 Ludwig Mies van der Rohe, Edith Farnsworth Residence, Plano, Illinois, 1945–1950. The Farnsworth Residence, with its all-glass curtain walls, was widely criticized for its lack of privacy.

[NOT SENT]

Dear Lewis:

Olgivanna has just read your *New Yorker* accolade to me.[1] Lewis—I now understand, for the first time, why you have never been to Taliesin, East or West, and that the old sore still rankles in your mind. The fatal difference between us seems to lie in everyone for the commonplace instead of the commonplace for everyone as something to rise above by his innate strength of inspiration.

Communism versus Democracy; quality above quantity? But no doubt now, you have blessed everyone but your victim which is what the critic usually considers his privilege, if not his sacred duty. The International Style wins. It seems to have found a friend in you. But I am really astonished to see you put the cart before the horse—giving the works of the Europeans precedence when it really belongs to us because of my work appearing there in 1910 (eleven years previous), which does not seem to interest you, for some reason.[2]

As for humanist-qualities, consider Broadacre-City again for just that. And—you might take a look at the Taliesin Fellowship itself for a valid humanitarian-impulse in my work, on my part, if so inclined.

As a matter of fact the humanities are dead against your judgements all down the line of your criticism. This will someday become even more evident. I believe.

Yes, the old quarrel comes uppermost again! How sad. Does the exercise of the critical-faculty require a bias of some kind? I never realized how little—in detail—you really "took-in" of my real significance as an architect to myself, to my time or to you and yours—in my work.

Nevertheless, my best to Sophie, Allison[*sic*] and yourself.

Affection as always, now from the Democrat to the Socialist, . . . now.

[signed]
Frank
Frank Lloyd Wright
December 18th, 1953

---

1 Mumford, "The Sky Line: A Phoenix Too Infrequent—II."

2 Wright, *Ausgeführte Bauten und Entwürfe von Frank Lloyd Wright*.

Llewis! What really hurts is to know that you—to whom I have looked with hope and love should understand my work so much in reverse.

[signed]
F.

[ts&ms flwa]

Dear Lewis:

Literature tells what happens to man but Architecture represents and presents it.

Affection,
Frank Lloyd Wright
December 18th, 1953

[cc ts flwa]

[VARIANT]

Dear Lewis:

Literature tells what happens to man but Architecture presents him.

N.B. You have stuck in a whole row of pegs for writers to hang their hats on.

Affection,
Frank Lloyd Wright
December 18th, 1953

[cc ts flwa]

1954–1958

In early 1954, Mumford attempts to balm the wounds he has caused in his friendship with Wright. A few months later, Wright commends Mumford for writing a letter to the *New York Times* protesting the Cold War. Sophia Mumford and Olgivanna Wright exchange letters in spring and fall that provide details of their personal lives.

Illness again prevents the Mumfords from visiting the Wrights in 1955 on the occasion of the architect's eighty-eighth birthday. Mumford indicates he is in the process of revising *Sticks and Stones*, "the book that first brought us together." When it is published later in the year, Wright calls it "admirable" and "brave." Olgivanna Wright publishes a book of her personal philosophy, *The Struggle Within*. In October 1956, Wright is honored by the City of Chicago. Mumford is asked to preside over an evening banquet, but tells Wright he cannot make room in his schedule, when in fact he is fuming over Wright's new project for a Skyscraper a Mile High.

Only a few letters are exchanged in 1957–1958. Wright is miffed by a piece written by Henry-Russell Hitchcock, Jr. Mumford writes of his projects, including a small booklet on Wright, as well as his new appointment at the Massachusetts Institute of Technology and his continued fears concerning the Cold War. Wright sends Mumford a revised chapter from his autobiography that reexamines his early years with Louis Sullivan.

THE DRAKE
SPRUCE STREET-WEST OF FIFTEENTH
PHILADELPHIA 2

4 JANUARY 1954

... The best of my Christmas presents didn't reach me till yesterday, when we came back from our holiday as a family in Amenia: they were your two letters, dear Frank, waiting mid a great batch of unforwarded mail. I couldn't ask for a happier New Year greeting. As for your work, it will remain long after anything I write about it and will have the last word. That is as it should be. "The best cannot be said: the best is that which remains unsaid." Happily, what I have written by way of criticism in these all-too-brief articles will make it easier to utter without reserve all the things that remain to be said about your work—and particularly about the beauties and glories of these climactic years, in the buildings I have yet to see with my own eyes.

Meanwhile, all power and light to you, and all blessings for the coming year, to you and yours. Sophy adds her affectionate good wishes to mine.

With gratitude for you large-heartedness
Ever yours
[signed]
Lewis

[ms flwa]

OLGIVANNA LLOYD WRIGHT

APRIL 2ND 1954

Dear Sophie,

I am sorry not to have been able to stay in New York to have lunch with you that day. But there was an urgent call from Iovanna who needed my immediate help—I had to go. You may have heard she gave the performance of dances in the Goodman theatre in Chicago.[1]

The young people had bad press reports but the audience was completely with them.

I shall always look forward to our being together again. What disagreements Lewis & Frank might have is entirely their own affair. We somehow correspond as families—the three of you and the three of us and the two that are missing.[2]

So I send all three of you my love and my wish that the goodness of life spares no gifts from you.

[signed]
Olgivanna

[pc ms lmp]

---

1 *Music, Ritual Exercises and Temple Dance by Georges Gurdjieff*, performance introduced by Frank Lloyd Wright and presented by members of the Taliesin Fellowship under the auspices of the Art Institute of Chicago, Goodman Theater, Chicago, 3 November 1953.

2 Geddes Mumford and Svetlana Wright Peters (1917–1946), daughter of Olgivanna Lloyd Wright, adopted daughter of Frank Lloyd Wright, and wife of William Wesley Peters. Svetlana Wright Peters was killed with her son Daniel in an automobile accident near Spring Green, Wisconsin in 1946.

Dear Lewis:

A clipping of your letter to the *Times* shows you back again on the trail so worthy of you—and you worthy of it.[1] A splendid courageous arraignment of gross stupidity in high places.

Affection,
[signed]
Frank
Frank Lloyd Wright
April 5th, 1954

[ts lmp]

1 Lewis Mumford, "Policy on [Hydrogen] Bomb Examined," *New York Times*, section IV (28 March 1954): 10.

MRS. LEWIS MUMFORD: AMENIA: NEW YORK

12 APRIL 1954

Dear Olgivanna:

Your letter warmed the hearts of us—all three, for Alison was home for spring vacation when it came, forwarded from New York where we no longer live. Except for the fall term at the University of Pennsylvania, we now live here in our beloved house. Though of course I was very sorry not to see you that day, I was glad to know that when your daughter wanted you, you dropped everything and went to her. I felt it another bond between us. Just as I feel, no matter how the words go between them, there is in both our husbands a recognition of quality in each other that transcends differences of opinion.

For ourselves, you and I, I still cherish a hope that sometime we will meet for more than a fleeting moment at luncheon. Always after we have been together I feel a deep well has been touched and I cherish our meetings. I wish they could be oftener and more prolonged. Perhaps some day Lewis and I will go West and you will be in Taliesin and we can see you there; I haven't given up that hope.

For the while, though, the warmest of greetings from house to house.

[signed]
Sophia

[ms flwa]

THE DRAKE
SPRUCE STREET-WEST OF FIFTEENTH
PHILADELPHIA 2

18 OCTOBER 1954

Dear Olgivanna:

We were both more than sorry that Lewis' teaching schedule kept him in Philadelphia and so we could not attend the welcoming party for you last week. We are pleased that you included us among the guests you wanted. It would have been very good to have had even the brief glimpse of you such an occasion would have afforded.

I had to make a short overnight trip to New York on Tuesday and I telephoned the Plaza hoping at least to talk with you over the phone as compensation, but they said you were not there. Alas.

All along I cherished the idea of seeing you this spring in Taliesin, but Lewis finds he must stay in Amenia when he finishes his stint here, to re-write a book he started last spring, and so he has cancelled the Western trip.[1] If I were not possessed of an incurable optimism I would despair of ever seeing you as I someday want to with enough time and proper circumstance so that we might truly be able to talk with one another. Patience may yet win out.

I hope all has gone very well with all of you and that Iovanna gets much joy of her work. After a two year lapse Alison began drawing this year. She has a talent and we are glad she is working at it again.

The warmest of greetings from house to house.

Always
[signed]
Sophia

[ms flwa]

---

1 Probably Lewis Mumford, *The Transformations of Man* (New York: Harper and Brothers, 1956).

AS OF
AMENIA, NEW YORK

2 JANUARY 1955

Dear F. Ll. W.:

Let this first letter of the New Year open with affectionate greetings from both of us to yourself and Olgivanna! For the last two months I have been waiting for a quiet moment to write you: but even the holiday at Amenia—I write from Philadelphia, where I shall be till February—did not provide it. Are you really coming to the East, to install yourself here? That would be good luck for us here: but I grieve over your leaving your lares & penates—knowing how keenly I'd regret leaving mine at Amenia, though they are only a generation old. Still, "where the MacGregor is, there is the head of the table" applies to you even more than the Scotch clans: the Wisconsin in you will be more real than the Wisconsin you are leaving behind.

Do let us know when you are back in New York again: we are both eager to see you. Meanwhile, our warm embraces.

Ever yours,
[signed]
Lewis

[ms flwa]

LEWIS MUMFORD
AMENIA, NEW YORK

1 JUNE 1955

Dear Olgivanna:

It was a joy to get your telegram this morning and it would have been a far deeper joy if we could accept your invitation.[1] If life had been kind to us this spring, it would have been the best possible time for a visit. By now, the book I was working on should have been done, and this would have been the first interlude in a year, with no demands and no pressures.[2] But alas! Sophia came down five weeks ago with a rare virus that kept her in the hospital three weeks; and after twelve days of high fever she's so weak that she has been in bed ever since coming home. The doctor doubts if she will be fully recovered before the summer is over. This has proved the worst illness of her life—almost a fatal one. Alison, unfortunately, will not be back here, to keep house till 10 June: so I cannot go out to Wisconsin alone, as I might have been tempted to for this occasion after a whole lifetime of postponements—even though my book is still far from finished. We are sad, for many reasons, that things are so: not least because we'd both like to reciprocate in person the love and understanding that shines through your message.

In deep friendship;
[signed]
Lewis

P.S. The enclosed is for Frank—for his birthday.

[ms flwa]

---

1 Telegram unlocated.
2 Probably Mumford, *The Transformations of Man*.

LEWIS MUMFORD
AMENIA, NEW YORK

1 JUNE 1955

Dear Frank:

Let me begin with an embrace for your birthday: an affectionate embrace in which Sophy joins me. We are desolate because it is impossible for us to be with you: nothing would have made us more happy than to swell in person the chorus that will greet you this day. As for you, one who has achieved immortality is beyond such vain punctuation marks as birthdays: it is we, who cannot fly at your side above the clouds, who note and count such dusty milestones. I called you, in *The Roots of [Contemporary] American Architecture*, "The Fujiyama of American Architecture"; for the perpetual volcano of your creativity has turned you into a sacred shrine: dominating the scene both by your works and your presence, and radiating your beneficent energy over us all. May we have a life long enough to enjoy all that you have imagined and built.... In revising Sticks & Stones—the book that first brought us together—I find that the task is largely a matter of adding, at appropriate points, your name![1]

All blessings, then, on your great life and on the day that celebrates it.

In love & friendship,
[signed]
Lewis Mumford

[ms flwa]

1 Lewis Mumford, *Sticks and Stones: A Study of American Architecture and Civilization*, rev. ed. (New York: Dover Publications, 1955).

OLGIVANNA LLOYD WRIGHT

JUNE 20TH 1955

Dear Lewis,

Frank and I missed having you, Sophia and Alison with us at Taliesin and we were very sorry to hear of the illness which kept you from coming. Sophia's strong nature should help her overcome the virus sooner than the doctors predict. They are not always right!

Frank was happy to have your beautiful letter on his birthday. We are both looking forward to your new book and we are especially pleased that "Sticks and Stones" is to appear again. It was the basis of your friendship with Frank because it came at the time when he needed support and you were among the first to give it to him.

The book on which I have been working is coming out in October. It is a series of philosophic essays—the result of my search, study and experiences in the realm of ideas.[1]

I hope that you and Sophia will find yourselves in harmony with what I have written. Anyway we always yearn that those we care for will understand us.

With my love to you,
[signed]
Olgivanna

[pc ms lmp]

---

1 Olgivanna Lloyd Wright, *The Struggle Within* (New York: Horizon Press, 1955).

[INSCRIPTION IN *Sticks and Stones*, REVISED EDITION]

For Frank: with love: the book that first brought us together.

[signed]
Lewis
Amenia, N.Y.
September 1955

[ms flwa]

Mr. Lewis Mumford
Amenia
New York

My dear Lewis:

So happy to see the important little book. It did bring us together. Admirable it is and (at that time) brave. I wish it might keep us there where we used to be. We see too little of each other, Lewis—so when again we arrive at our Plaza place let's all get together for argument in old fashion.

We hope you, your Sophie and your daughter are as happy as your thought of me makes us.

Affection as always,
Frank Lloyd Wright
October 19th, 1955

N.B. Why have you never seen "the Taliesins" nor their equivalents?

[cc ts flwa]

MRS. LEWIS MUMFORD
AMENIA, NEW YORK

1 JANUARY 1956

Dear Olgivanna:

Not the least of the joys attendant on opening this house for the holidays was to find your book waiting for us. We came back only just in time to welcome home Alison and her future husband, Rob Cowley, and my niece and her new husband, so that the time has gone by in a whirl of planning and talking and much young enthusiasm—all lovely but time-consuming.[1] Now the house is half-emptied and the other half asleep and for the moment there is peace and quiet in which to say thank you, not only for the gift of *The Struggle Within*, but for the wisdom it contains. For so long I have cherished the hope of some time spending a quiet hour with you—now in a measure that wish is fulfilled. Doubly I welcome it because it follows the questions raised by some of the young ones who visited here and I can share its insights with them. I have not finally read it—it is a book to come back to and slowly to absorb—there is so much life wisdom in it: and so distilled that it is accessible to those it can benefit.

Again, dear Olgivanna, my thanks to you for having written it and for having sent it.

Our love to you both.
[signed]
Sophia

[ms flwa]

1 Robert W. Cowley (b. 1934), American writer and editor.

LEWIS MUMFORD
AMENIA, NEW YORK

17 MAY 1956

Dear Olgivanna Wright:

If only we could come to Taliesin for Frank's birthday! Nothing would give us more joy—except the very event that prevents it: Alison's graduation from Radcliffe. It was good of you to renew the invitation: our thoughts will be with you both on that brave day,

Affectionate good wishes
[signed]
Lewis

[ms flwa]

LEWIS MUMFORD
AMENIA, NEW YORK

7 OCTOBER 1956

Dear Frank:

As you must have known when we talked together, my immediate impulse was to say yes for the great occasion on the seventeenth.[1] But the three days I would have to give, to make that evening possible, would make it impossible for me to write the Introduction to the French monograph on your work, before leaving the country in November: so I decided—though sadly—that writing the Introduction was more important than being chairman.[2] If I'd known of the occasion earlier I could have arranged things different.

... How good it must feel—though tinged with irony—to find yourself honored fully at last in your own country!

With affectionate greetings
Ever yours
[signed]
Lewis

[ms flwa]

---

1 Mayor Richard Daley proclaimed 17 October 1956 as "Frank Lloyd Wright Day in Chicago." Mumford is referring to the culminating evening banquet at the Hotel Sherman.
2 Mumford evidently never wrote this introduction.

Dear Lewis:

Sophie is right.

No sooner had I finished asking you to preside at the Frank Lloyd Wright Day big Chicago banquet than I realized I had asked something you should not do if you would preserve your status as a professional critic.

So, anticipating your refusal, I invited Dr. Ludd M. Spivey, President of Florida Southern.[1] He well knows what it is all about and is free to preside without compromise or being compromised. He is competent and skillful. I hope you know the spirit in which I proposed your leadership on the occasion. It was purely fraternal.

Convey my respects to your Sophie and my admiration in the circumstances.

Faithfully,
Frank Lloyd Wright
October 10th, 1956

[cc ts flwa]

---

1 Ludd M. Spivey (1886–1962); Frank Lloyd Wright, Florida Southern College, Lakeland, Florida, 1938–57.

Mr. Lewis Mumford
Amenia
New York

Dear Lewis:

"As one master to another"—a note: to have my work reviewed by an Internationalist is like having "The Sermon on the Mount" reviewed by an atheist?

Daughter Iovanna, herself developing into a poetic writer said of Hitchcock's review in the *Times*, "Daddy, it smells bad right from the start."[1]

Affection,
Frank Lloyd Wright
November 20th, 1957

[cc ts flwa]

---

1 Henry-Russell Hitchcock, Jr., "Architecture and the Architect," review of *A Testament*, by Frank Lloyd Wright, *New York Times Book Review* (17 November 1957): 44.

14 FRANCIS AVENUE
CAMBRIDGE 38, MASS.

5 DEC. 1957

. . . Your letter, dear Frank, crossed one I had been writing in my mind for the last couple of weeks, and, what with the aftermath of the flu and one thing and another, had not yet written. You mustn't be too disappointed about Hitchcock: he "knows all about architecture," but unfortunately he lacks the capacity to feel it and understand it; and that failing is a particularly grave one in dealing with your work. This is the academic disease that now spreads like dry rot through all the arts.

My special reason for writing you is this. My Italian friend, Mario Labo, who translated the *Culture of Cities*, is editing a series of little books on architecture, mostly illustrations with only a few pages of text.[1] He would like me to do the book on you; and, though this doesn't fall in easily with my plans, this is both an honor and an opportunity I could not lightly refuse. But I have not yet accepted, definitely, because I wouldn't like to undertake the job unless it had your blessing; and unless I could count on your help in getting photos or photostats of your work, as many as 60 or 80. If you'd rather someone else were invited to do the job, do not hesitate to say so. They want an American to write the introduction or they would doubtless have called on Zevi; but if you'd prefer that Manson did it, I'll gladly hand on his name, or that of anyone else you'd prefer, to Labo.[2]

Sophy and I are here at Cambridge till the end of January: then back to Amenia, where I shall, if all goes well, start work on a new book.[3] As a visiting professor at M.I.T. I am treated with the respect usually accorded a first class mathematician or physicist: that is, I am left to myself, with no other duties than a two-hour seminar a week.[4] These would be very happy days, if it weren't for the underlying con-

---

1 Mario Labo (1884–1961), Italian writer and editor. Mumford evidently never wrote this introduction.

2 Grant Carpenter Manson (1904–1997), American architectural historian.

3 Probably Lewis Mumford, *The City in History: Its Origins, Its Transformations, and Its Prospects* (New York: Harcourt, Brace and Company, 1961).

4 Mumford was a visiting professor at the Massachusetts Institute of Technology between 1957 and 1961.

viction that our leaders in Washington, with their imbecile strategy of extermination, are grimly committed to our national suicide; and except for a few people like Omar Bradley and myself, no one seems to understand that our life now hangs by a thread, and will continue so to hang until we dismantle our whole sinister apparatus, and address ourselves to saving the human race from destruction.[5] But it will take guts as well as brains to retreat from the Cold War and to overcome our delusions of moral and technological superiority; and both guts and brains are lacking in the places where they would make the most difference in Washington. I've just been down there and found that those who best understand these dangers don't dare whisper about them in public.

Sophy joins me in an affectionate embrace with Olgivanna and you—

Ever yours
[signed]
Lewis

[ts&ms flwa]

5 Omar Bradley (1893–1981), U.S. Army general.

[C. DECEMBER 1957]

Dear Llewis:

Good news. Agreement all down the line. Nothing would please me more than to have you back on your old line—seeing in instead of at. "Sticks and Stones" was prophetic at a crucial time. Now a Sticks and Stones again might save us another quarter of a century of the cliché—the cliché seems fated to barge in on organic integrity and as conformity increases.

What you feel about our loss of our national character of the free leader of the free world is true and there now is "the frontier." You are welcome to choose what you will from the mass of material now at Taliesin and I suggest you come there to go through it with me to find a coherent series telling the story beyond modern architecture by some time.

Say when and all shall be at your service because of all the surveyors of organic architecture you best know the meaning of "Nature" and "Organic"—from which the drift away has again "set in."

To you and yours, Llewis—

Affection—
Frank Lloyd Wright

N.B. I will send you a few leaves lately written for the loose-leaf Autobiography on the matter now seeming to interest the critic on the relationship of L.H.S. and F.Ll.W.[1]

[cc ts flwa]

---

1 Louis Henry Sullivan; Frank Lloyd Wright, unpublished revisions to *An Autobiography*, flwa, AV#2401.384.

Dear Llewis:
Here is the chapter to which I referred.[1] Kindly read and return?

It is all I shall ever have to say on the subject and as true as I can make it.

Merry Christmas to you and yours—

and affection,
Frank Lloyd Wright
December 24th, 1957

[cc ts flwa]

1 See previous letter, note 1.

AS OF
AMENIA, NEW YORK

1 JANUARY 1958
(AFTER 1 FEB.)

. . . I have yet to thank you, dear Frank, for your Testament and for the inscription within it: so let me begin the New Year with these thanks & with an affectionate embrace.[1] May the New Year keep you in health and bring to even richer fulfillment all your works. Your blessing on my doing the little Italian book on your work naturally delights me: and if it's at all possible I'll run out to Taliesin for the pictures and a further look around. Meanwhile Sophy joins me in warm greetings to you & Olgivanna.

[signed]
Lewis

[ms flwa]

1 Frank Lloyd Wright, *A Testament* (New York: Horizon Press, [1957]); inscription unlocated.

AS OF
AMENIA, NEW YORK

3 JANUARY 1958

Dear Frank:

I read this as soon as the postman brought it, and I don't think a word should be added or taken away. It is both just and merciful, appreciative & critical; and that is what the present generation needs to know about Sullivan. Many people have taken Sullivan's interpretation of his failure as a full explanation of it: but I had only to read his *Kindergarten Chats* to realize that this was far from the whole truth.[1] Except perhaps in his relations with you at the end of his life, he seems to have been incapable of love. His contempt for his draughtsman extends to the imaginary pupil in *K.C.* Perhaps this was the familiar psychological dodge for evading his own contempt for himself, for having betrayed his own talents, whoring and drinking. You said enough to put the right key in the hands of a perceptive reader without saying too much. Your analysis of Sullivan's use of clay forms is classic; that limitation of his, apart from anything else, would define the difference between you.

Thank you for letting me see this.

And again a Happy New Year!

Affectionately
[signed]
Lewis

[ms flwa]

1 Louis H. Sullivan, *Kindergarten Chats* (Lawrence, Kansas: Scarab Fraternity Press, 1934).

Dear Lewis:

Olgivanna and I have often discussed the fact that the Mumfords have never honoured either of the Taliesins with a sojourn—of any kind. Why is this true? I have no answer. In truth, there is none explicable—or ethical—so it must be moral? Now that daughter is married and if Sophie were reconciled, you too may be comparatively free to roam—why do we not plan a few days going over auld lang syne and see what we at Taliesin have ploughed into this valley—a choice example of what Southern Wisconsin would be like were no poles and wires along the valley-roads, the right kind of buildings for the right kind of people in the right places.... and how liberally all this adds up to humanity in possession of its birthright.

You would be completely by yourselves to carry on whatever work you desired, for as long or short a time as the spirit claimed.

We would take care of any expense incurred because of a talk or two with the friendly youth inhabiting part of Taliesin—this as you might decide would be merely incidental or not at all.

We have growing pains and are badly oversized. Your views on the young college of Architecture my will is establishing would be especially welcome to me at this time.

My best to you both in the way of affection and appreciation,

[signed]
Frank
Frank Lloyd Wright
May 22nd, 1958

[pc ts lmp]

[INSCRIPTION IN *The Human Way Out*[1]]

For Frank & Olgivanna
in friendship

[signed]
Lewis
Amenia, N.Y.
29 May 1958

[ms flwa]

1 Lewis Mumford, *The Human Way Out* (Wallingford, Pennsylvania: Pendle Hill, 1958).

[NOT SENT]

Lieber Llewis:

Vegetables to you—my man! Here I find myself again on the opposite side of the "offense." Llewis—there is nothing either of us can do about "young." (Like vegetables). Youth is a quality good at thirty-six, sixty—better at ninety or a hundred, or civilization fails. Youth is spirit! If you have lived well above the belt, according to creation, you will not die young but better—youthful and that may be your immortality? So the creative-spirit hath decreed! Believe me, there is nothing I cannot do better now than ever—but less and less of it. Since I never had enough to do at any time there seems not to be too much now as I keenly enjoy it all or do not wish to do it. I wish the same for you, my friend of the "young" days.

Llewis, by nature and training, the socialist versus the American individualist to the "sovereignty of the Individual" to his fellow creator, American socialist—

Llewis, don't be a dear old mule—I am beginning to feel that you are afraid of me: afraid you might lose some of the cherished beliefs regarding attitudes, predilections, affections and predetermined philosophy of mankind: don't want to expose yourself to contamination—or argument?

But I know there must be some other cause of absence—some other reason less egotistic and futile. I understand a man's absorption in his work to the exclusion of any honor he might bestow upon an old friend by his presence. But this absenteeism I fear has other causes into which I will do well not to "dig." Even if I could and how can I?

Salute! Dear Llewis: Yours shall remain a cherished secret—incognito, insofar as our fellowship goes.

Don't grieve about Allison [*sic*] because she is so lucky to have "found-out" soon enough.[1] There are innumerable discretions as well as indiscretions ahead for young Allison as for our Iovanna.

My level best to your handsome, intelligent wife, Sophie, and as for you, "lieber Llewis"—look out for the ingrowing of a special talent amounting to genius.

1 Wright refers to Alison Jane Mumford's broken engagement to Robert Cowley.

Affection,
Frank Lloyd Wright
June 4th, 1958

N.B.
Hokusai was ninety-seven and prayed for three years more—if granted, "every dot and every line would be alive."[2] Hiroshige, seventy and then some. All the big old philosophers had white beards hanging below the level of the navel and I have now duly "rapped on wood"—the cross.—Three times—. Here are a few statistics in the region of the vegetable:—and thrown in. Bernard Shaw a hundred but for a fall from an apple tree—Etc. Etc. Youth is a quality, young is a circumstance.

[ts&ms flwa]

2 Katsushika Hokusai (1760–1849), Japanese artist whose woodblock prints were a major part of Wright's art collection.

Dear Llewis:

Don't be a dear old mule—I am beginning to feel that you are afraid of me: afraid you might lose some of the cherished beliefs regarding attitudes, predilections, affections and predetermined philosophy of mankind: don't want to expose yourself to contamination—or argument?

But I know there must be some other cause of absence—some other reason less egotistic and futile. I understand a man's absorption in his work to the exclusion of any honor he might bestow upon an old friend by his presence. But this absenteeism I fear has other causes into which I will do well not to "dig." Even if I could, how can I?

Salute! dear Llewis: yours shall remain a cherished secret—incognito in so far as our fellowship goes.

Don't grieve about Allison [*sic*] because she is so lucky to have "found-out" soon enough. There are innumerable discretions as well as indiscretions ahead for your Allison as for our Iovanna.

My level best to your handsome, intelligent wife, Sophie, and as for you, "lieber Llewis"—look out for the ingrowing of a special talent amounting to genius.

Affection,
[signed]
Frank
Frank Lloyd Wright
June 4th, 1958

[pc ts lmp]

[NOT SENT]

Dear Lewis: On reflection!

There is one difference between creator and craftsman: the more a creator does the more creative he becomes as he grows in practice, whereas the more the artisan does the less he can do as his work-life increases. The reason for this lies in the nature of the human-Spirit. The craftsman is fed by the creator.

The creator is inspired by a source—Nature. He knows no limit—its reality. Age is to him but a qualification. His vision grows or diminishes by its exercise.

Affection,
[signed]
Frank FLLW
Frank Lloyd Wright
August 27th, 1958

[ts&ms flwa]

1959

News of Wright's death in April reaches the Mumfords in Philadelphia, where they are in residence at the University of Pennsylvania. Sophia and Lewis individually send their condolences to Olgivanna Wright. Lewis reminds Olgivanna of her own important role during her husband's most productive years. Olgivanna responds with a wish that there had been even more good words between the two men.

3414 SANSOM STREET.
PHILADELPHIA 4, PENNA.

12 APRIL 1959.

Dear Olgivanna:

I somehow believe you know my heart is with you these dreadful days. You must face now the moment we all hope to escape, those of us who are on the far side of the hill. But I know you will find in your courageous soul the path to lead you on, alone after so many years of vibrant companionship—of living two as one, now left alone to carry the life of two. I don't speak of the world's loss—for who is there to carry his particular contribution on?—but for you and with you I mourn deeply. My heart is with you.

Always,
[signed]
Sophia (Mumford)

[ms flwa]

AS OF
AMENIA, NEW YORK

15 APRIL 1959

. . . What can I say by way of love and sympathy at this moment that you do not already know in your heart? Your loss is our loss: yet the two are incommensurable. The great period of Frank's life was that which followed his marriage with you: all that led up to this, however magnificent, was still preparatory. Be consoled by the thought of all that you did that helped to make those years so fecund and memorable. Let this lift you in your grief, as it lifts us who have no claim to such intimacy.

Last Monday—I am writing to you from the University of Pennsylvania—I was scheduled to give a lecture on Modern Architecture: instead I spoke for almost two hours on Frank. The students, on the day the sad news came over the radio, had flown a black streamer from the flagpole at the School of Fine Arts: and they turned out, as never before, to do honor to him at the lecture. He filled their thoughts, one of them told me, all that night.

When you come East, dear Olgivanna, I trust you will visit us. In the meanwhile, our tenderest sympathy.

Ever yours,
[signed]
Lewis Mumford

[ms flwa]

OLGIVANNA LLOYD WRIGHT

May 9th, 1959

Dear Lewis

Thank you for your letter—your words are good. I wish there were more of them to Frank himself when he was alive—he felt badly over your relationship. It is sad that so often death opens the eyes of the living.

With affection to you and Sophia,

[signed]
Olgivanna

[pc ms lmp]

Chronology

FRANK LLOYD WRIGHT[1]

1867 Born on June 8 in Richland Center, Wisconsin.
1876 Introduced by his mother to the Froebel kindergarten training system.
1886 Enters University of Wisconsin's School of Civil Engineering.
1887 Arrives in Chicago; works for Joseph Lyman Silsbee.
1888 Works for Adler and Sullivan, Chicago.
1889 Marries Catherine Lee Tobin.
1893 Leaves Adler and Sullivan; opens own architectural office in Chicago.
1901 Designs projects "A Home in a Prairie Town" and "A Small House with 'Lots of Room in It'" for the Curtis Publishing Company.
1908 Writes "In the Cause of Architecture" for the *Architectural Record*; designs Frederick C. Robie Residence in Chicago.
1909 Leaves wife and children to sail for Europe with Mamah Borthwick Cheney to prepare work for publication by Ernst Wasmuth in Berlin.
1910 Returns to United States; *Ausgeführte Bauten und Entwürfe von Frank Lloyd Wright* published by Ernst Wasmuth.
1911 Revisits Europe; begins construction of Taliesin, a rural retreat near Spring Green, Wisconsin.
1914 Publishes "In the Cause of Architecture, Second Paper" in the *Architectural Record*. Seven people, including Mamah and her two children are murdered by a servant at Taliesin; living quarters are set afire. Meets Miriam Noel and begins rebuilding Taliesin.
1916 Receives commission for Imperial Hotel, Tokyo, Japan; construction begins three years later.

---

1 In compiling this chronology, I am indebted to several authors and scholars, including Anthony Alofsin, Penny Fowler, Grant Carpenter Manson, Oskär R. Muñoz, Peter S. Reed, Margo Stipe, and Robert L. Sweeney. Their research and assistance have made this work possible—BBP.

1922 Receives divorce from Catherine Wright.

1923 Major earthquake strikes Tokyo; innovative design of Imperial Hotel prevents all but minor damage. Marries Miriam Noel.

1924 Separates from Miriam Wright; introduced to Olgivanna Lazovich Hinzenberg in Chicago.

1925 Publication of *Wendingen* special issue, *The Life-Work of the American Architect Frank Lloyd Wright*. Olgivanna and daughter Svetlana move into Taliesin; fire again consumes living quarters at Taliesin. Daughter Iovanna is born in December to Wright and Hinzenberg.

1926 Initiates correspondence with Lewis Mumford in August. Bank of Wisconsin takes possession of Taliesin. Wright and Hinzenberg arrested and jailed briefly on Mann Act charge in Hennipen County, Minnesota.

1927 Begins writing series, "In the Cause of Architecture," for the *Architectural Record*. Mann Act charges dropped; receives divorce from Miriam Wright.

1928 Evicted from Taliesin by Bank of Wisconsin; visits Phoenix, Arizona. Marries Hinzenberg at Rancho Santa Fe, California and soon after adopts Svetlana.

1929 Regains control of Taliesin. Builds desert camp, "Ocotilla," while at work on commissions in Arizona.

1930 Lectures at Princeton University. Exhibition of his work begins national tour; international venues added in 1931.

1931 *Modern Architecture: Being the Kahn Lectures for 1930* published; judges Columbus Memorial Lighthouse competition in Brazil.

1932 Participates in *Modern Architecture: International Exhibition* at the Museum of Modern Art, New York; publishes *An Autobiography* and *The Disappearing City*; launches "The Taliesin Fellowship," an architecture school at Taliesin, in October.

1934 Begins work on "Broadacre City" model.

1935 Moves with his family and the Fellowship to Arizona; finishes Broadacre City model, which subsequently tours the United States; designs the Edgar J. Kaufmann Residence ("Fallingwater"), near Mill Run, Pennsylvania.

1936 Designs S. C. Johnson & Son Headquarters Building, Racine, Wisconsin.

1937 Begins construction of Taliesin West in Scottsdale, Arizona, a winter home for the Fellowship.

1938 *Architectural Forum* devotes January issue to Wright's work; appears on cover of *Time* in January.

1940 Featured in *Two Great Americans: Frank Lloyd Wright and D. W. Griffith* at the Museum of Modern Art, New York; Frank Lloyd Wright Foundation is incorporated.

1941 *Frank Lloyd Wright on Architecture*, edited by Frederick Gutheim, is published; awarded gold medal of the Royal Institute of British Architects on the approval of King George VI; breaks relations with Mumford over Mumford's interventionist stance.

1943 Revises and expands *An Autobiography*; receives commission for the Solomon R. Guggenheim Museum, New York.

1946 Daughter Svetlana killed in automobile accident.

1948 *Architectural Forum* again devotes entire issue to Wright's work in January.
1949 Publishes *Genius and the Mobocracy*; receives gold medal from the American Institute of Architects.
1951 For a third time, the *Architectural Forum* devotes January issue to Wright's work. Exhibition *Sixty Years of Living Architecture* opens at Gimbel's Department Store, Philadelphia and subsequently travels to Florence and other European and American venues. De Medici Medal conferred by the City of Florence at the Palazzo Vecchio; Star of Solidarity awarded by the State of Italy and presented by Count Carlo Sforza, in the Doge's Palace, Venice; receives gold medal of the American Academy of Arts and Letters. Wright and Mumford resume their correspondence at Wright's initiative.
1952 Fire destroys major portion of Hillside Home School building at Taliesin, including theater and dining room; rebuilt almost immediately.
1953 Publishes *The Future of Architecture*.
1954 Establishes apartment and office in Plaza Hotel, New York while at work on the Solomon R. Guggenheim Museum; publishes *The Natural House*.
1955 Publishes *An American Architecture*, edited by Edgar J. Kaufmann, Jr.
1956 "Frank Lloyd Wright Day" proclaimed in Chicago by Mayor Richard Daley on October 17; project for "A Skyscraper, A Mile High" unveiled; publishes *The Story of the Tower*.
1957 Publishes *A Testament*; interviewed on ABC television by Mike Wallace.
1958 Publishes *The Living City*; suffers slight stroke early in summer but recovers by summer's end; writes last letter to Lewis Mumford in August.
1959 Dies on April 9 in Phoenix, Arizona.

LEWIS MUMFORD[2]

1895 Born on October 19 in Flushing, Long Island.
1912 Graduates from Stuyvesant High School; matriculates at the City College of New York.
1914 Reads works by Patrick Geddes; leaves City College.
1918 Enlists in U.S. Navy.
1919 Discharged from U.S. Navy; begins career as journalist and critic.
1921 Marries Sophia Wittenberg, former colleague on the staff of the *Dial*.
1922 Publishes *The Story of Utopias*.
1924 Publishes *Sticks and Stones*, translated into German the following year.
1925 Son Geddes is born; moves to Sunnyside Gardens, Long Island City, Queens. Lectures at International Summer School, Geneva, Switzerland. Writes first essay about Frank Lloyd Wright for *Wendingen*.
1926 Publishes *The Golden Day*. Rents summer cottage in Leedsville, near Amenia, New York. Exchanges letters with Frank Lloyd Wright.

---

2 I am indebted to Mumford's biographer, Donald A. Miller, in compiling this chronology—RW.

1927 Meets Frank Lloyd Wright for the first time over lunch at Plaza Hotel; makes first visit to Chicago area to view Wright's architecture in person.

1929 Publishes *Herman Melville*; begins visiting professorship at Dartmouth College.

1930 Purchases farmhouse in Leedsville, New York as summer retreat.

1931 Publishes *The Brown Decades*; appointed architecture critic of the *New Yorker* in charge of "The Sky Line" column.

1932 Writes "Housing" essay for *Modern Architecture: International Exhibition* at the Museum of Modern Art, New York; rejects Wright's offer to lead the Taliesin Fellowship; studies modern architecture in Europe.

1934 Publishes *Technics and Civilization*, volume one of The Renewal of Life.

1935 Daughter Alison Jane is born. Reviews Wright's Broadacre City for the *New Yorker*.

1936 Moves with his family permanently to the farmhouse in Leedsville, New York.

1938 Publishes *The Culture of Cities*, volume two of The Renewal of Life; appears on cover of *Time* in April.

1939 Publishes *Men Must Act*; urges U.S. involvement on side of Allies in World War II.

1941 Breaks relations with Frank Lloyd Wright over the architect's isolationist stance.

1942 Joins faculty of Stanford University.

1944 Son Geddes killed in combat; publishes *The Condition of Man*, volume three of The Renewal of Life; resigns from Stanford University.

1947 Publishes *Green Memories*, a biography of Geddes Mumford.

1951 Publishes *The Conduct of Life*, volume four of The Renewal of Life; begins visiting professorship at the University of Pennsylvania; resumes correspondence with Frank Lloyd Wright.

1952 Edits *Roots of Contemporary American Architecture*, including essay "The Art and Craft of the Machine," by Frank Lloyd Wright. Meets Wright at Plaza Hotel, New York, in February for reunion luncheon.

1953 Publishes two-part profile of Frank Lloyd Wright in the *New Yorker*.

1955 Publishes revised editions of *Sticks and Stones* and *The Brown Decades*.

1956 Publishes *The Transformations of Man*.

1959 Lectures extemporaneously on Frank Lloyd Wright at the University of Pennsylvania upon hearing of the architect's death; reviews the Solomon R. Guggenheim Museum for the *New Yorker*.

1961 Publishes *The City in History*, which wins the National Book Award for nonfiction the next year.

1963 Retires as architecture critic for the *New Yorker*.

1967 Publishes *The Myth of the Machine: I. Technics and Human Development*.

1970 Publishes *The Myth of the Machine: II. The Pentagon of Power*.

1982 Publishes *Sketches from Life*, an autobiography covering the first half of his life.

1990 Dies on January 26 at his home in Leedsville, New York.

Index